Decades of our Lives

60s

Decades of our Lives

CLASSIC, RARE, AND UNSEEN 60s

FROM THE ARCHIVES OF THE DAILY MAIL

Trans
Atlantic
Press

This was the swinging decade when the postwar "baby boomers" came of age. They found themselves in a new permissive era as the Pill launched a sexual revolution. Hemlines rose; all you needed was love, according to pop icons the Beatles. The flower power counterculture challenged the old orthodoxies; student riots in Paris encapsulated the mood of protest that was abroad. John F. Kennedy carried the hopes of a generation when he was elected US president in 1960, and although his vision to put a man on the moon was realized, he didn't live to see it. Martin Luther King also fell to an assassin's bullet, a shattering blow to the civil rights

movement. The Berlin Wall went up, Nelson Mandela began his long period of incarceration and the Cold War temperature plummeted as the superpowers played high-stakes geopolitics in Vietnam. Muhammad Ali was jailed for draft-dodging but remained the sporting colossus of the day. The hovercraft and Concorde made their debuts, while Christiaan Barnard pushed back the medical frontier by performing the first heart transplant.
From the momentous and the apocalyptic to the offbeat and the trivial, the photographs in this book, from the archives of the *Daily Mail*, chart the people, places, and events that made up a memorable decade.

1960

In the 1950s the ideal of feminine beauty was Doris Day, and girls read comics at happy sleepovers with nightgowns buttoned to the neck. As the 60s progressed everything changed.

ABOVE: Female telephone operators at work. Telephone calls were connected manually but as the decade wore on, electronic switchboards began to take over. Some homes were still connected by a party line where several households shared a phone line so would need to take it in turns to make a call.

OPPOSITE: The manual typewriter was the key office machine in the 1960s, a heavy, noisy, and relatively slow device but in the right hands much faster than writing, though not shorthand, that other important office technology. E. Remington & Sons exercised a US patent and adopted the QWERTY keyboard around 1873; with a few additions, the 1960s manual wasn't too different. By the end of the decade the electric typewriter was making life much easier, IBM Selectrics were the state of the art, and the days of courier 12 point were numbered.

The Sharpeville shootings took place in South Africa in March when over 5,000 people gathered to protest about the pass laws that the government used as part of its apartheid rule. Black Africans had to carry the pass book to show they had permission to travel in "white" South Africa. The protesters offered themselves for arrest at Sharpeville police station for not carrying their pass books. Armored vehicles were called in to confront the crowd and the armed police opened fire with machine guns, killing 69 and wounding another 180. Sharpeville was the catalyst that turned peaceful protest to armed militant resistance, resulting in the banning of the ANC and the beginning of South Africa's isolation from the international community.

The nuclear age created great anxiety about the threat of atomic weapons. In the UK in 1958 CND organized the first march from Aldermaston, site of Britain's Atomic Weapons Research Establishment; the march ended in a large public rally in Trafalgar Square and the event was held each Easter weekend until 1963 when an international test ban treaty was signed. CND stood for the Campaign for Nuclear Disarmament and its logo, designed by Gerald Holtom, became the universal symbol for peace and disarmament; never copyrighted, CND allowed the symbol to be freely used around the world.

LEFT: Movie star and director John Wayne pictured before the premiere of *The Alamo* in 1960. Wayne was later nominated for an Oscar as the producer of Best Picture for the movie about the 1863 Battle of the Alamo, one of two films he directed in his long career. The other was *The Green Berets* in 1968, the only major movie made during the Vietnam War which supported the conflict.

OPPOSITE: Anthony Perkins as Norman Bates and Janet Leigh in the role of Marion Crane in the classic Hitchcock thriller *Psycho*. Crane is on the run with money stolen from her boss and checks into the Bates Motel. Unfortunately she doesn't spot that the good looking young owner is a murderous psychopath. The movie performed well at the box office and received four Oscar nominations. The shower scene became a defining moment in cinematic tension and the movie is considered one of Hitchcock's best.

OPPOSITE: On September, 16, 1960, at Bonneville Salt Flats, USA, Donald Campbell sought to follow in his father's steps by setting a new land speed record. He pushed his turbine-powered car, *Bluebird*, to an incredible 365 mph before crashing on his second run, sustaining a fractured skull and various minor injuries. The car was destroyed and after being rebuilt in 1962 was shipped to Australia, where, at Lake Eyre in 1964, an undeterred Campbell would pilot *Bluebird* to a new land speed record of 403.1 mph.

RIGHT: Stirling Moss (center) ended an otherwise frustrating Formula One season in 1960 with a win in the United States at Riverside. Graham Hill (right) had an even more disappointing season: he finished only one race all year in his BRM.

ABOVE: Newlyweds Yul and Doris Brynner in Mexico; they married while shooting *The Magnificent Seven* (1960) and are seen here flanked by stars of the movie (pictured left to right): Charles Bronson, Eli Walach, Horst Buchholz, Brad Dexter, and Steve McQueen. The movie was based upon Akira Kurosawa's brilliant *Seven Samurai* (1954). The latest Brynner marriage was less enduring than the movie and they divorced in 1967.

OPPOSITE: By the end of the 1950s rock and roll was no longer just the music of teenage rebellion. In 1960, pop stars such as Adam Faith and Cliff Richard projected themselves as responsible and clean living members of society. Here teenage singer Adam Faith poses for a portrait by society photographer Archie Parker.

ABOVE: Jawaharlal Nehru (right) talks with US President Dwight Eisenhower in New York. Nehru was India's first prime Minister; educated in England at Harrow and Trinity College, Cambridge, while still a young man Nehru campaigned for India's independence from the UK taking lead of the left wing of the Indian National Congress. When independence was finally achieved, he was chosen to create the political reality that Mahatma Gandhi had envisioned and struggled for. "Ike" was nearly at the end of his second term as president and was the first to be denied a third term under constitutional reforms instituted by Harry S. Truman.

OPPOSITE: British Prime Minister Harold MacMillan in deep conversation with President Josip Tito of Yugoslavia while in New York for the United Nations General Assembly. Tito led the Yugoslavian resistance during Nazi occupation and became the country's first Prime Minister. Although he formed a communist regime and followed the Soviet model, Tito kept independence and was able to maintain open international relations. With Nehru of India, Nasser of Egypt, and the leaders of Indonesia and Ghana—all emergent nations—Tito set up the Non-Aligned Movement and became its first Secretary General in 1961.

OPPOSITE: Tony Hancock (right) and Sid James appearing in one of the television episodes of *Hancock's Half Hour*. The show, written by Ray Galton and Alan Simpson, originated as a groundbreaking BBC radio comedy which first aired in 1954. Tony Hancock starred as an exaggerated version of himself, a down-at-heel comedian trying to hit the big time while struggling to make ends meet at 23 Railway Cuttings, East Cheam. Sid James played the role of the roguish friend who usually managed to get the better of his unfortunate pal.

ABOVE: The Everly Brothers, April 1960. Phil (left) and Don Everly were an American pop duo who transformed the bluegrass sound of their Kentucky boyhood into a richly harmonized form of rock and roll. Their close harmony singing had a strong influence on many of the rock and roll performers of the early 1960s. In 1960 their single "Cathy's Clown" sold eight million copies worldwide and topped the US *Billboard*

1960

OPPOSITE: The Queen's sister, Princess Margaret, and husband, photographer Antony Armstrong-Jones, seen in public with newly born David, later Viscount Linley. When the Queen elevated Armstrong-Jones to Earl of Snowdon in 1961, Princess Margaret added the title Countess of Snowdon.

RIGHT: Nine-year-old Princess Anne attends Badminton Horse trials with brother Charles and Queen Elizabeth II in April 1960. The Princess developed an interest in horses from a very early age and later went on to take part in the 1976 Olympic Games in Montreal as a member of the British team, riding the Queen's horse, Goodwill.

ABOVE: Paul Newman and wife Joanne Woodward. Newman had just completed filming *Exodus* on location in Cyprus. In the same year *From the Terrace* was released, in which Newman and Woodward starred together. They married in 1958 and remained together until 2008 when Newman died. In all they appeared in 10 feature films together.

OPPOSITE: Following the success of *The Magnificent Seven*, Steve McQueen got top billing in *The Honeymoon Machine*. He is pictured with Paula Prentiss and Brigid Bazlen, co-stars in the movie.

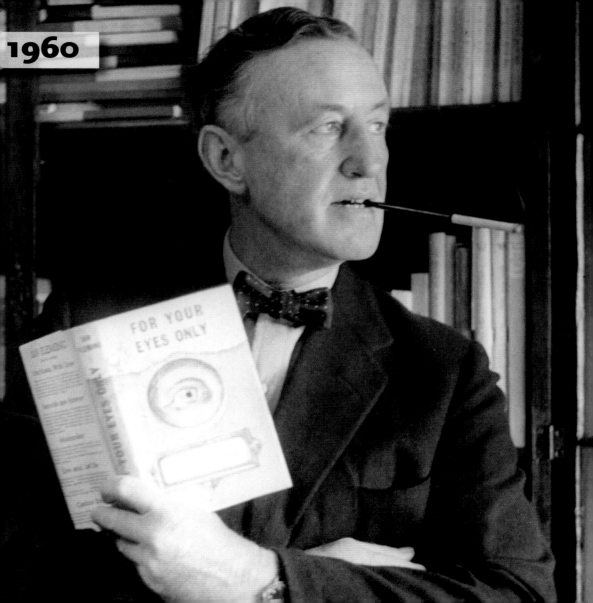

1960

ABOVE: Artist L. S. Lowry at work in his home in November 1960. The painter became famous for his depictions of life in the industrial quarters of England's northern cities in the early 20th century. His distinctive style of painting is best known for urban landscapes featuring human figures often referred to as "matchstick men."

OPPOSITE: English author Ian Fleming in his study, holding the eighth in his series of 14 James Bond books, two of which were published after his death. Like his hero, Fleming was born an upper class Englishman and served in naval intelligence through World War II. Published by Jonathan Cape in 1960, *For Your Eyes Only* was a collection of five short stories including *From a View to a Kill, For Your Eyes Only* and *Quantum of Solace*—titles that would become familiar to future generations of movie-goers.

1960

ABOVE: At the 1960 Olympic Games, Rome, Wilma Rudolph sets a new Olympic record of 23.2 secs in the opening women's 200 meters heat; USA's Rudolph went on to win the gold medal.

OPPOSITE: Ethiopian Abebe Bikila wins the Olympic marathon in 1960. Bikila was a last minute substitute for the injured team member Wami Biratu; he ran barefoot because the running shoes supplied by sponsor Adidas were uncomfortable; in any case, Bikila had trained barefoot. Warned by his team trainer to look out for number 26, he did not know that Moroccan Rhadi Ben Abdesselam wa wearing the wrong number of 185 and after working his way up the field still had not passed number 26. Only when he finished 26 seconds ahead of Rhadi did he find out the truth. Bikila's international marathon career continued and he returned to win a second gold medal in the 1964 Olympics

1960

ABOVE: Filming on the set of the ill-fated movie *Cleopatra* at Pinewood studios in November 1960. Beset with a series of disasters, the film nearly bankrupted 20th Century Fox; actress Elizabeth Taylor was cast in the title role, but became seriously ill early on in filming, which contributed to an already delayed schedule. The production then had to be relocated to Rome to help Taylor's recovery and the elaborate sets, which in England kept being damaged by bad weather, were rebuilt. During filming, Elizabeth Taylor began a very public affair with co-star Richard Burton, which made headlines worldwide.

OPPOSITE: Shirley MacLaine and Jack Lemmon star in Billy Wilder's movie, *The Apartment*. The picture won five Oscars including Best Movie and was nominated for a further five.

1960

OPPOSITE: American composer and conductor Leonard Bernstein in rehearsal. In 1960 Bernstein began the first complete recording of Mahler's nine symphonies: an interesting counterpoint to his musical *West Side Story*, based on Shakespeare's play *Romeo and Juliet*. At this time *West Side Story* was in the middle of a three-year run in London's West End. After a brief break touring the USA in 1960, the US production returned to Broadway for another 253 performances—a total of over 1,000 at Manhattan's Winter Garden Theater. In 1961 the movie production and a very successful soundtrack would introduce the opera to a new audience.

ABOVE: Rodgers and Hammerstein in March 1960, seen here signing autographs for enthusiastic fans. Librettist Oscar Hammerstein II is first on the left, Richard Rodgers at the table next to him. Together they composed some of the most successful musicals ever, including *The Sound of Music*, which was running on Broadway at the time of this photograph; they were also responsible for *Oklahoma!*, *Carousel*, *South Pacific*, and *The King and I*. Hammerstein died of stomach cancer in the summer of 1960.

1960

LEFT: Maria Bueno of Brazil in action at the Wimbledon Lawn Tennis Championships, June 23, 1960. For the second year in a row, Bueno took the Women's Singles title at Wimbledon, beating South African Sandra Reynolds Price in the final. Partnered with American Darlene Hard, she also won the Ladies' Doubles title at the tournament.

OPPOSITE: Wolverhampton Wanderers return home with the FA Cup after beating Blackburn Rovers 3–0 in the final at Wembley in May 1960. Triumphant captain Bill Slater (left) proudly holds the cup aloft as they make their way to a celebratory reception. Slater's FA Cup medal was the crowning glory in a career in which he won three Football League Championship medals and 12 England caps. Later in the year he went on to win the Footballer of the Year title for the 1959–60 season.

1961

JFK and Jackie. When President Kennedy was elected in 1960 at the age of 43, he became the youngest-ever US president; with his glamorous wife, Kennedy appeared to embody the promise of a belief in youthful idealism and optimism, as epitomized in his inaugural speech when he made his famous declaration, "Ask not what your country can do for you; ask what you can do for your country."

ABOVE: Soldiers clear the snow from seats in front of the Capitol in Washington, D.C., in preparation for the inauguration of John Kennedy as the 35th President of the USA in January.

OPPOSITE: The third generation Ford Thunderbird was unveiled to an eager market in 1961. Already a popular model, the Thunderbird evoked power and freedom to the style-conscious driver who either had a second, family car or was still free of dependents and able to enjoy the call of the open road. Its status as the car of young, forward-looking Americans was confirmed with its appearance in President Kennedy's inaugural parade. Ford was brought closer to the hub of government when one of its senior executives, Robert McNamara, was made Secretary of Defense.

1961

ABOVE: Australian Rod Laver holds the Wimbledon Men's Singles Cup in July 1961. Laver was probably the best male tennis player of the 1960s and was the only player to win the Grand Slam first as an amateur and again as a professional. He won Wimbledon four times: in 1961 and 1962 as an amateur and, after turning professional and being banned, returning in 1968 to win the first two open championships.

OPPOSITE: Tottenham Hotspur and Northern Ireland football captain Danny Blanchflower was happy enough to be celebrated on the football pitch, here holding the FA Cup aloft after beating Leicester City in the 1961 final, giving them the league and cup "double" triumph. However, he surprised the British public when he refused to appear on TV's *This Is Your Life*. He found it difficult to explain his reasons for refusing to participate in what was one of the most popular programs in 1961.

OPPOSITE: Nelson Mandela and his wife Winnie enjoy a happy moment. The next three decades would have little levity for Mandela, who became leader of the militant wing of the African National Congress, known as the MK, in 1961. After the Sharpeville shootings, Mandela led a campaign of sabotage against the government and its military, with the intention of avoiding killing people. Mandela was arrested the following year and was sent to jail until his release in 1990.

RIGHT: President Charles de Gaulle of France inspects the guard of honor on his arrival in Britain for talks with British Prime Minister Harold Macmillan. De Gaulle was credited with keeping Britain out of the European Economic Community (EEC) or Common Market since its inception in 1957, prompting Britain to devise the rival European Free Trade Association (EFTA) in 1959. By 1961 Britain was attempting to persuade the EEC to allow EFTA to join the Common Market, but de Gaulle vetoed this.

1961

ABOVE: Having been a successful stage production both sides of the Atlantic, *West Side Story* was released as a movie in October 1961. Hailed as a great artistic success, it won 10 out of its 11 Academy Award nominations, including Best Film.

OPPOSITE: Marcello Mastroianni plays opposite Anita Ekberg in a scene from *La Dolce Vita*, director Federico Fellini's masterpiece. Released in Italy in 1960 to mixed reaction—largely because of its religious parodies and overt sexuality—it was released to US audiences in 1961 and received praise from the *New York Times*. The movie won the Palme d'Or at Cannes and an Academy Award for Best Costume.

RIGHT: The historic first meeting of Soviet Prime Minister Nikita Khrushchev and President John F. Kennedy at the American ambassador's residence in Vienna in June 1961. In October of the following year the two were to be major players in the Cuban Missile Crisis which brought the world to the brink of nuclear war.

OPPOSITE: Kennedy's term of presidency at the height of the Cold War was turbulent and he needed his diplomatic allies; he and British Prime Minister Harold Macmillan pose for the cameras at a break during talks in Bermuda, where they met to discuss world affairs, including civil unrest in the Congo and the threat of the continuing Cold War.

1961

Babe Ruth's single-season home run record, set in 1927, falls when Roger Maris hits his 61st off the Red Sox's Tracy Stallard on the last day of the season.

RIGHT: Jimmy Hill turns out for Fulham FC. In 1961 Hill was the Chairman of the Professional Footballers' Association (the players' union) and led negotiations that abolished the maximum wage for footballers, allowing the top players to demand more for their talents. Injury put paid to any chance of a long career and instead Jimmy Hill went on to become the face of football on television throughout the 1970s and 1980s.

OPPOSITE: The legendary Stanley Matthews warms up before the match in which his team, Stoke City, beat Chelsea. Matthews returned to Stoke in 1961, toward the end of a phenomenal career which he had begun there as a schoolboy. By 1965, aged 50, Matthews was the oldest player in the Football League, and in 33 years had never been booked. That year he would also become the first footballer to be knighted.

1961

ABOVE: Television became hugely popular during the 1960s and while concerns were voiced over the quality of of broadcasts, particularly those of commercial television companies, the public generally welcomed the increased provision of so-called "light entertainment." Host of *Take Your Pick*, Michael Miles, is pictured here with Mrs. Emily Ayerst, who tried unsuccessfully to win a trip of a lifetime on the popular quiz show. Viewers were so touched by her desire to see her son in Australia that their donations, and P&O's gift of a free return sea passage, enabled her to make the trip.

OPPOSITE: Actor Richard Chamberlain in his TV role as Dr. Kildare in the series of the same name.

1961

OPPOSITE: The Twist was a long-lasting dance craze that was to prove a classic. Songs like Chubby Checker's "Let's Twist Again" got couples and singles onto the dance floor with few steps to learn. Watched here by some suspicious French citizens, a pair of British youngsters take part in a twisting competition on the dock at Calais, France. They crossed the channel on the *Royal Daffodil*, spent three hours twisting in France, and then returned to Britain.

ABOVE: The Twist crossed all generation divides; here a group of schoolchildren perform the dance in the street.

1961

LEFT: While Europe was still emerging from post-war austerity, New York was viewed as a Christmas-reveler's dream: here the Fifth Avenue snowflake lights up one of the greatest shopping streets in the world.

OPPOSITE: The Macy's Thanksgiving Day parade in New York City began as a tradition in 1924. The six and a half mile route had its starting point in Harlem and ended in Herald Square, location of Macy's main entrance on Broadway. A key feature from 1927 was giant balloons of Disney and other well-known characters—Popeye, seen here, first appeared in 1957. Televised across the USA, the hour-long broadcast gained massive audiences and in 1961 was doubled to two hours.

In August 1961 Michael Gregsten and Valerie Storie were hijacked at gunpoint during an illicit meeting in Gregsten's car. Michael Hanratty was identified by Storie as the murderer of Gregsten during the nighttime drive that took them to Deadman's Hill on the A6 road north of St. Albans, near London; she was raped and shot but survived. Here policemen are stopping drivers in an attempt to gather information. The murder weapon would turn up two days after the crime under the seat of a London bus. Hanratty's conviction during the infamous "A6 murder trial" was called into question by a number of famous people, notably John Lennon, but that would not stop Hanratty from being among the last few criminals to be hanged in Britain.

Nazi war criminal Adolf Eichmann stands trial in Jerusalem in 1961. Tracked down and captured by the Mossad in Argentina, where he had lived under a false identity since 1950, Eichmann's trial was broadcast around the world. He played a pivotal role in the holocaust, responsible for the logistics of transporting Jews around Europe to and from ghettos and the extermination camps. After 14 weeks in court Eichmann was found guilty on all charges and was hanged in May the following year.

ABOVE: In 1961 Soviet-controled East Germany erected a barrier, completely surrounding West Berlin, known as the Berlin Wall; all population movement crossing this boundary was under military control. Here East German policemen are seen discussing the border situation and politics with West Berliners through barbed wire at sector border Wildenbruchstrasse in District Neukoelin, Berlin. On the left of the picture East German soldiers are carrying materials to build the wall.

OPPOSITE: The presence of the Berlin Wall in front of the Brandenburg Gate, a strong German national symbol, was a daily reminder of the occupation, domination, and division of the German nation.

1961

ABOVE: Margaret Thatcher's first ministerial appointment came in 1961 when she became a parliamentary secretary to the Ministry of Pensions and National Insurance. She is pictured reading her eight-year-old twins Carol and Mark a bedtime story.

OPPOSITE: Queen Elizabeth II rides on an elephant during the royal tour of Nepal in February and March 1961. The Queen and Prince Philip attended a tiger shoot arranged for them by King Mahendra of Nepal in a jungle near Katmandu. The Duke of Edinburgh was prevented from taking part in the shoot by a whitlow infection of his trigger finger.

1961

Mary Tyler Moore and Dick Van Dyke play a married couple in multiple Emmy award winning US TV sitcom *The Dick Van Dyke Show*, which went behind the scenes of a fictional TV show whose host was loosely based on comic actor and leadman Sid Caesar; after all, TV was the new hot medium, rapidly expanding in the 1960s. The show ran from 1961 to 1966 over a total of 158 episodes.

OPPOSITE: The Irish-bred Nicolaus Silver winning the 1961 Grand National at Aintree racecourse. He was the first gray to win the prestigious race since 1868. The first official Grand National was held at Aintree in 1839 when the aptly named Lottery won the race. In those days the horses had to jump over a stone wall, cross a stretch of plowed land, and clear two hurdles.

RIGHT: "The Maestro," Fulham footballer Johnny Haynes, leaves the field. The English inside forward played nearly 600 games and scored over 150 goals for Fulham Football Club between 1952 and 1970. He was particularly noted for his exceptional passing skill and ability to read a game. Haynes became the first player to be paid £100 a week immediately following the abolition of the £20 maximum wage in 1961.

An early experimental hovercraft, designed by Christopher Cockerell, is tested on the River Thames, London, in the early 1960s. Cockerell had begun work on developing the hovercraft in the early 1950s but had not been able to find a commerical sponsor. His ideas were eventually taken up by the National Research Development Council, which helped to finance the construction of the Saunders-Roe—Nautical One pictured here.

Coronation Street is one of the longest-running television programs in the UK. Set in the fictional town of Weatherfield in Greater Manchester, the popular soap focused on the lives of the street's residents. In this early episode, busybody battleaxe Ena Sharples (played by Violet Carson) is pictured having an argument and a scuffle with bumbling retail manager Leonard Swindley (Arthur Lowe).

ABOVE: Arnold Palmer makes his Ryder Cup debut in the 14th tournament, which was held at the Royal Lytham & St Annes Golf Club in 1961. The biennial competition between Europe and the United States was won by the US with a score of 14^1/$_2$ to 9^1/$_2$ points—a higher combined total than usual because a change in the competition format meant that the number of games had doubled, and so had the number of points available.

OPPOSITE: Wrestler Jackie "Mr. TV" Pallo demonstrates the Japanese leg lock on his unfortunate opponent. Pallo was a star of British televised wrestling in its 1960s and 1970s heyday and was one of the best known wrestlers of his era. In the bouts which were regularly televised on Saturday afternoons, he became a popular villain, known for his devious tricks in the ring.

1961

ABOVE: The northern gate of the Workers' Stadium in Beijing, 1961. This multipurpose stadium was built in 1959 for the 10th anniversary of founding of the People's Republic of China. One of its early functions was to host the first National Sports Meet, and in recent years it has seen all manner of sporting and cultural events, including pop concerts and soccer matches, including the 2008 Beijing Olympics soccer semifinals.

OPPOSITE: Chairman Mao Zedong photographed at the time of the five-year plan known as "the Great Leap Forward." Launched in 1959, the planned economy consolidated huge agricultural collectives which also had small scale industrial production; when rice harvests declined significantly, party officials failed to report true figures and the rural producers were forced to supply the political center and to export, leaving the farming collectives virtually to starve. Millions died and Zedong was forced to end the initiative in 1962.

1961

LEFT: In 1961 Audrey Hepburn played one of her most famous roles as Holly Golightly in Blake Edward's movie *Breakfast at Tiffany's*. George Peppard played opposite her, complementing Hepburn's character, whose ingenuous yet chic persona became an icon of the 60s. Hepburn performed the movie's keynote song, "Moon River," herself; it was composed by Henry Mancini specifically to accommodate her vocal range.

OPPOSITE: Walter Brown stars as gamekeeper Mellors with Jeanne Moody as Lady Chatterley in the play of D. H. Lawrence's infamous novel, *Lady Chatterley's Lover*. The publication of the book caused a scandal due to its explicit sex scenes and previously banned four-letter words. The publishers, Penguin Books, were tried and acquitted in Britain under the Obscene Publications Act. Following this dramatic and much publicized trial, bookshops all over the country sold out of the unexpurgated version of the novel on the first day of its distribution.

ABOVE: A Cuban airliner is ablaze after being hit by a rocket fired by a raiding aircraft over the airport at Santiago during the invasion of Cuba. The "Bay of Pigs" invasion was an unsuccessful attempt by American-backed Cuban rebels to invade southern Cuba and overthrow the Soviet-supported government of Fidel Castro. The plan was launched in April 1961, less than three months after John F. Kennedy was inaugurated as the 35th President of the United States.

OPPOSITE: From the 1950s into the 1960s there was a mass migration of workers from all over the English-speaking Caribbean into Britain. The British government was keen to recruit the immigrants into areas of labor shortages such as London's transport system and the National Health Service. For their part, the immigrants believed that Britain promised them the opportunity of a higher standard of living with a chance to earn wages that would enable them to send money back home to their families.

1962

Astronaut John Glenn boards
the *Friendship 7* space capsule
prior to takeoff on February 20,
to become the first American
to orbit the earth during the
Mercury-Atlas 6 mission. Glenn
completed three orbits in just
under five hours, splashing
down in the Atlantic Ocean to be
recovered by USS *Noa*.

ABOVE: The Queen shakes hands with Cliff Richard in the foyer at the London Palladium after the Royal Command Performance on October 29, 1962. Cliff would soon be back at the top of the charts for three weeks with "Bachelor Boy." To Richard's left is Rosemary Clooney and to his right, Harry Secombe and Eartha Kitt.

OPPOSITE: Wilfred Brambell (left) and Harry H. Corbett pose with Hercules the horse in advance of a new comedy series, *Steptoe and Son*. Originally produced in black and white from 1962 to 1965, the show returned in color in 1970, and ran for another four series until 1974, also spawning two spin-off movies and the highly successful NBC TV adaptation, *Sanford and Son*.

1962

Hollywood icon Marilyn Monroe captures President John F. Kennedy's ear while Attorney General Robert Kennedy looks on, studiously ignoring Arthur Schlesinger, Jr. The occasion was an after-party hosted by Arthur Krim, President of United Artists. Earlier in the evening Monroe had herself sewn into a stunning $5,000 rhinestone-encrusted dress to appear very belatedly at a celebration concert at Madison Square Garden, New York City, marking the President's birthday. First she sang "Happy Birthday" then segued into a special verse written by Richard Adler to the tune of "Thanks for the Memory". Her demeanour, the song, and the dress spelled out confirmation of the rumor that had become widespread: Monroe was the lover of one, or both, of the Kennedy brothers. She was months away from her death.

ABOVE: Fitted kitchen units in simulated teak with pale gray marble-effect plastic work tops teamed with crimson, saffron, and sapphire Paisley pattern wallpaper and blind are the height of fashion in this display from the 1962 Ideal Home Exhibition.

OPPOSITE: The 1962 Ideal Home Exhibition shows all the latest in kitchen design, including a built-in oven and counter hotplate. The kitchen's color scheme is sunshine yellow and white.

62

OPPOSITE: Fashionable hairdresser Vidal Sassoon of Bond Street, London, puts the finishing touches to the hair of singer Miss Denney Dayviss. The "beehive" hairdo, which was very popular during the 1960s, was achieved by backcombing the hair until it resembled candy floss and then smoothing the top strands over.

RIGHT: Swedish model Berit Ramsten poses in a Youthcraft Tidy Tab panty girdle and bra. Although panty girdles had been around since the 1930s they only became popular in the 1960s when panty hose started to replace stockings. Women's underwear also began to emphasize the breasts instead of the waist, and the decade saw the introduction of the bullet bra pointed bust, inspired by Christian Dior's "New Look."

ABOVE: At a meeting of the National Revolutionary Militia in Havana, Castro promises "No gratuitous attacks and no gratuitous hostile acts" against the United States.

OPPOSITE: Demonstrators stage a sit-in in Trafalgar Square, London, protesting the blockade of Cuba.

1962

OPPOSITE: Images of young, "beautiful people" heralded new definitions of social status based on fashion and lifestyle, led by designers, pop and movie stars, artists, models, and the like. Among the most famous faces of the swinging sixties was model Jean Shrimpton, "the Shrimp," a favorite of the photographer David Bailey.

RIGHT: Italian movie star Sophia Loren, born Sofia Scicolone in Rome in 1934, rose to fame in Italy during the 1950s and by 1960 had been taken up by Hollywood. In 1961 she starred in *El Cid* with Charlton Heston and the same year won an Oscar for her performance in *Two Women*. *The Millionairess*, a 1960 British movie in which she starred with Peter Sellers, resulted in a chart-topping single, "Goodness Gracious Me," produced by George Martin, in which Loren and Sellers performed the song in the voices of their film characters.

1962

ABOVE: Shirley Anne Field with Steve McQueen and Robert Wagner during the filming of *The War Lover*, a 1962 drama directed by Philip Leacock and loosely based on a Pulitzer-winning novel by John Hersey. McQueen plays maverick Flying Fortress captain Buzz Rickson, based in the east of England during the Second World War.

OPPOSITE: American star Judy Garland pictured with British actor Dirk Bogarde in 1962. They were to appear together in *I Could Go on Singing* (1963), for which they received high praise; Bogarde took on rewrites of Garland's lines in filming and the planned original title of the movie was changed so audiences would understand that Garland was returning to a singing role in a movie for the first time since 1954's *A Star Is Born*. Ironically perhaps, *I Could Go on Singing* was to be Judy Garland's last movie.

1962

ABOVE: Powerful men gather: Lord Beaverbrook sits between Sir Winston Churchill and British Prime Minister Harold Macmillan. Born William Maxwell Aitken in Ontario in 1879, the son of a Scottish Presbyterian minister, he moved to Britain, became a Conservative MP, and was granted the title of Lord Beaverbrook by David Lloyd George in 1918. During the First World War he acquired a controlling interest in the *Daily Express* and turned the paper into the most widely read newspaper in the world. He later founded the *Sunday Express* and in 1929 purchased the *London Evening Standard*.

OPPOSITE: Former US President General Dwight Eisenhower chats with former British Prime Minister Clement Attlee at a luncheon in Eisenhower's honor at the Savoy Hotel, London.

1962

OPPOSITE: John Wells, William Rushton, Richard Ingrams, and Barbara Windsor make an early appearance together in a late night cabaret show. English cartoonist and comedian Willie Rushton was a co-founder of the satirical news magazine *Private Eye* with former schoolmates Richard Ingrams and Paul Foot. Although at first *Private Eye* was little more than an extension of their school magazine, its reputation for biting satire and unexpected revelations about politicians and social figures often meant the magazine broke news stories that more established media dared not release.

ABOVE: Much of television programing was unsophisticated by today's standards, as shown above. However, July 1962 saw the first publicly available live transatlantic television broadcast, via Telstar 1, featuring CBS's Walter Cronkite and NBC's Chet Huntley in New York, and the BBC's Richard Dimbleby in Brussels, as well as footage of a baseball match and President Kennedy's press conference about the dollar.

1962

LEFT: Philadelphia Warriors' Wilt Chamberlain leaps to score in a game against the New York Knicks. On March 2 in Hershey, Pennsylvannia, Chamberlain made a record score of 100 points against the Knicks; his 1961–62 season was his third in the NBA and brought the 7 foot 1 inch "Wilt the Stilt" to legendary fame as he became one of the highest scoring players of all time. His feats were not confined to the boards: he played in the movie *Conan the Destroyer*, was a successful businessman, and in his autobiography claimed to have enjoyed the favors of 20,000 women.

OPPOSITE: British road racing cyclist Tommy Simpson leads Belgian world champion Van Looy in the ninth stage of the 1962 Tour de France. He became the first Briton both to wear the leader's yellow jersey and to finish in the top 10 of the Tour de France. Simpson died on the slopes of Mont Ventoux while taking part in the 1967 Tour de France. The postmortem found that he had taken a combination of drugs which proved fatal when combined with the heat and the arduous climb of the mountain.

1962

ABOVE: The Star United Kingdom Ballroom Championship at the Albert Hall, London. The 1960s was a pivotal decade in dance as the arrival of rock and roll music meant that young people moved away from "formal" dancing with prescribed sequences of movements toward the more relaxed and casual style of solo or non-contact dances.

OPPOSITE: Singer Cliff Richard pictured at the London Transport Driving School in Chiswick, where he prepared for his role in the British musical film *Summer Holiday*, released in February 1963. The movie followed a group of friends as they drove across Europe in a double-decker bus and was another huge box office hit for the star after his 1961 success with his first major role in *The Young Ones*.

1963

A small expectant crowd gathers outside Liverpool's Cavern Club, home of the Mersey sound and above all the Mecca of Beatlemania, which rapidly gathered momentum during 1963.

1963

ABOVE: 1963 was the big year for the emerging Beatles; ceaseless touring around the UK and Europe was only interrupted by interviews, photocalls, and studio appearances like this pictured. Amid their hectic touring they achieved four hit singles and released two albums. At the beginning of the year they were supporting big name headliners such as Helen Shapiro and Chris Montez but by the end of the year they were the UK's top band.

OPPOSITE: Peter Yarrow, Mary Travers, and Paul Stookey, together the New York folk ensemble Peter, Paul, and Mary. By 1963 they had recorded three successful albums of what were to become folk standards, from Bob Dylan's "The Times They Are a-Changin" to covers of Pete Seeger songs such as "If I Had a Hammer." Their own hit, "Puff the Magic Dragon," raised suspicions of drug references but it was a song about lost childhood. Peter, Paul, and Mary smoothed the rough edge of folk music of the time with their sweet sound but their protest was clear when they performed at the famous civil rights march in Washington where Martin Luther King gave his most famous speech.

1963

OPPOSITE: Any time, anywhere: students on a Florida beach do the twist. Beach culture was boosted by the phenomenal success of the Californian band The Beach Boys, formed in 1961, who released three studio albums in 1963, making their Surf Sound one of the keynote musical genres of the 1960s.

RIGHT: Jack Lemmon pictured with his new wife actress Felicia Farr. Lemmon's previous marriage to Cynthia Stone lasted just six years but he remained married to Felicia until his death in 2001. *Days of Wine and Roses*, the first movie of three he made with Blake Edwards, was released in 1962; in it he played an alcoholic businessman—a role, he confessed later, that was closer to his personal situation at the time than anyone knew.

1963

OPPOSITE: President John F. Kennedy at his desk in the Oval Office. Kennedy's tenure in the White House spanned turbulent times, with Cold War tensions coming to the USA's front door in Cuba and the growing strength of the civil rights movement. At the same time organized crime held great power and was believed to have infiltrated the labor unions. Against this complex backdrop, JFK's assassination in November spawned many conspiracy theories.

ABOVE: President and Jackie Kennedy pictured leaving Love Field shortly after their arrival in Dallas, Texas, on November 22. When the President's motorcade passed through Dealey Plaza around 12:30 p.m. three shots were fired, mortally wounding him and severely wounding the Governor of Texas, John Connally. Vice-President Lyndon B. Johnson was sworn in as President on *Air Force 1* two hours after JFK was shot and within a week had appointed the Warren Commission to investigate the assassination; the Commission concluded that Lee Harvey Oswald was solely responsible for the shooting. Oswald himself was shot and killed by Jack Ruby before he could be put on trial.

1963

OPPOSITE: British MP John Profumo with his wife, former actress Valerie Hobson. Profumo was appointed Secretary of State for War in 1960. While at a party hosted by Viscount Astor he met model and society girl Christine Keeler and embarked on a brief affair with her. In 1962 it came to light that Keeler had also had a relationship with a senior naval attaché at the Soviet Embassy. In 1963 the scandal broke and Profumo initially denied impropriety but finally confessed and resigned from office and Parliament. The scandal rocked British politics and did great damage to the ruling Conservative government.

ABOVE: Mandy Rice-Davies is Miss Austin at the 1960 motor show that launched the Austin Seven Countryman, which later became known as the Mini Countryman. Over 100,000 were built. Rice-Davies, like Christine Keeler, was a member of the social set created by Dr. Stephen Ward, who was put on trial for living off their immoral earnings. It was clear to the public that the Profumo Affair was just one aspect of a wider sex scandal involving call girls.

ABOVE: James Garner and Donald Pleasance make a bid for freedom in the 1963 movie *The Great Escape*, based on Paul Brickhill's World War II book of the same name, which novelized a true story of a mass breakout from Nazi prisoner of war camp Stalag Luft III. The movie also starred Steve McQueen and Richard Attenborough.

OPPOSITE: Michael Caine pictured in the apartment that he shared with fellow actor Terence Stamp in 1963, the year that he got his first major film role in *Zulu*, for which he received excellent reviews.

1963

OPPOSITE: The Pan Am building, the world's largest commercial office building in 1963. Despite enormous engineering challenges created by construction over New York's main railway terminal, Grand Central Station, the 59 story building was completed on time. Architects Emery Roth & Sons received the assistance of Walter Gropius and Pietro Belluschi.

ABOVE: Jack Lemmon as the predatory landlord of a Californian apartment building in the comedy movie *Under the Yum Yum Tree*. Lemmon is pictured here in Ford Motor Company's concept car, the futuristic-looking Cougar 406, presented at the 1962 Chicago Motor Show; the car had electrically operated gullwing doors and a highly powerful V8 engine.

French actress Brigitte Bardot on location for the filming of *The Adorable Beast*. The same year she shocked audiences by appearing naked and reclining in the opening scene of *Contempt*. Bardot's personal life was as interesting and complex as her movies. Iconic photos circulated during the 1960s making her one of the world's greatest ever sex symbols.

American jazz musician and bandleader Duke Ellington relaxes with a music score in his hotel room while on tour. Between record labels in the early 1960s, Ellington was able to broaden his musical horizons by recording with other artists new to him. His extensive touring delighted his international fans and assured his position as the leading jazz musician of his age.

1963

| E. MORTIMER | T. ADES | O. JAMES | D. WICKHAM |

BALLIOL·OXFORD

| B. CLARK | D. MILLS | N. FOGG | A. BRIGNELL |

NOTTINGHAM

ABOVE: British TV quiz program *University Challenge* was launched in 1962, hosted by quizmaster Bamber Gascoigne. Based on the US series *College Bowl*, the cream of university intellects were matched against each other in intense half-hour competitions. The first final of the series was won by Leicester University in 1963.

OPPOSITE: Michael Landon in his popular role as Little Joe Cartwright in the long-running NBC TV series *Bonanza*, set on the Ponderosa, a large ranch in Nevada, USA. Joe was the youngest of three sons and his impetuous character combined with his fresh, handsome features won him many fans. Landon used his charms on the studio, persuading them he should be allowed to write episodes for the series—which he did, successfully continuing to write other shows after *Bonanza* ended.

ABOVE: Living conditions in some parts of the north of England were far from luxurious in the early 1960s and in this photograph appear little changed from when these terraces were first built. This woman washes the step into the backyard of her house in Bolton, Lancashire. Through the 1960s, steady economic improvement relieved some women of the burden of domestic toil with devices such as automatic washing machines and many other labor-saving appliances that made life easier and provided more time for leisure and relaxation.

OPPOSITE: In the 1960s not all households could afford their own washing machine—or had the space for drying clothes; the traditional wash-house, like public baths, was replaced by 24 hour self-service launderettes like this one in London in the 1960s. The world's first launderette, called a washteria, was opened in Fort Worth, Texas, in 1934. Machines could wash, rinse, and spin in a single automatic operation, unlike the twin tub machines that were more common in Europe during the 1960s.

1963

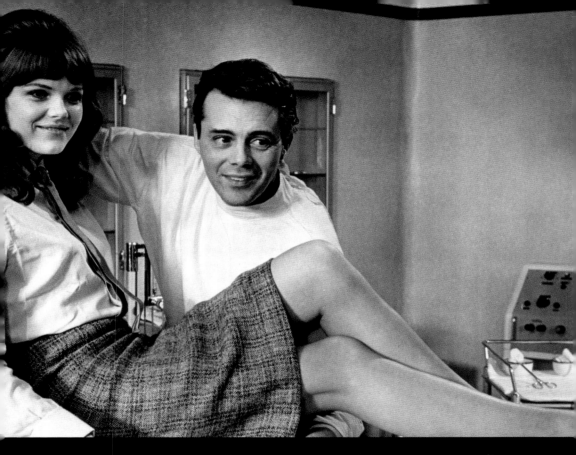

OPPOSITE: Elvis Presley and Joan O'Brien play nurse and patient in director Norman Taurog's film *It Happened at the World's Fair*. Set against the backdrop of the Seattle World Fair, the movie was a showcase for Presley's music which was released simultaneously as an LP. Here the young cropduster inveigles his way into the attentions of the resident nurse and main love interest!

ABOVE: Dirk Bogarde appears with Samanatha Eggar in a scene from the 1963 comedy film *Doctor in Distress*. This was his fourth appearance as Dr. Simon Sparrow in the series of Doctor films. Soon after this, the suave matinee idol abandoned his comedy heart-throb persona for more demanding and challenging roles and was awarded two BAFTAs for Best Actor in *Accident* in 1963 and *Darling* in 1965.

1963

LEFT: The Reverend Richard Wayne Penniman, known by the stage name Little Richard, is considered a key figure in the transition from rhythm and blues to rock and roll in the 1950s, due to his explosive music and charismatic persona. The flamboyant American singer and songwriter had a string of groundbreaking hit singles which influenced many future rock and roll artists including the Beatles, who were his support act in Germany and in his UK tours before they became even more famous than him.

OPPOSITE: American vocal group the Four Seasons—Frankie Valli, Bob Gaudio, Tommy de Vito, Nick Massi—were one of the most long-lived and successful white musical acts of the 1960s. The band became internationally famous with a series of smash hit singles between 1962 and 1967 featuring the distinctive falsetto voice of Frankie Valli backed by the close harmony vocals of the rest of the group.

OPPOSITE: Liverpool-born Gerry Marsden and his band Gerry and the Pacemakers were part of the Merseybeat sound of the early 1960s and the band was the second group signed by Beatles manager Brian Epstein. Marsden and his band are probably most remembered for the song "You'll Never Walk Alone," which has been adopted as an anthem of several football clubs, the most notable being Liverpool FC, the club Marsden supports.

ABOVE: Roy Kinnear, Kenneth Cope, David Frost, Willie Rushton, and Lance Percival get into comedy mode for the new satirical television show *That Was The Week That Was*. This was a show unlike any seen before and soon gained a reputation for savage satire and irreverence. Each week it was introduced by sophisticated jazz singer Millicent Martin performing the theme tune, with words altered to reflect the week's news, before going into a topical monologue by host David Frost. At the end of each episode Frost famously signed off with the line: "That was the week, that was."

HAROLD

OPPOSITE: British MP Harold Wilson, wearing his trademark raincoat, receives a kiss from wife Mary after he is elected leader of the Labour party in 1963. The following year he led the party to his first election victory and served as Prime Minister of the United Kingdom from 1964 to 1970, and again from 1974 to 1976, winning four out of the five general elections that he contested.

ABOVE: Britain's most notorious crime of the 1960s, the Great Train Robbery, took place in August 1963 when a gang of 15 criminals stole £2.6m from the night mail train from Glasgow to London. Gang member James White took refuge with his wife in a caravan in Surrey. Realizing the police were on their trail, they hid £35,000 behind the paneling in the caravan and in the tires, then fled from the site. Police systematically took the caravan to pieces, finally locating the cash. Thirteen of the gang members were eventually captured and convicted. Most of the stolen money was never recovered.

1963

RIGHT: Leeds United manager Don Revie leads Johnny Giles away from Old Trafford after signing the transfer agreement from Manchester United to Leeds. Giles had begun his professional football career at Old Trafford playing alongside Bobby Charlton and Denis Law, helping them secure the FA Cup in 1963. Shortly afterwards Giles requested a transfer and for a £33,000 fee joined their rivals. He began playing for the Republic of Ireland four days before his 19th birthday and made 59 appearances for his national side.

OPPOSITE: Brazilian soccer star Edison Arantes do Nascimento, popularly known as Pele, looks cheerful as he arrives in London with the Brazilian soccer team for an international against England at Wembley in May 1963. Pelé was a member of three World Cup winning teams and scored over 1,000 goals in his career.

1963

Peter Sellers in his much-loved role of Chief Inspector Clouseau in one of many farcical moments—this one with his "wife," played by Capucine—in Blake Edwards' comedy, *The Pink Panther*.

1963

ABOVE: On December 26, 1963, 12 inches of snow covered most of southern England. A week later the worst blizzard to hit Britain for 15 years brought London Airport to a standstill. Snowdrifts up to 30 feet deep blocked roads and railways, brought down power lines and left many isolated villages cut off. For three months temperatures barely rose above freezing, with nighttime temperatures falling as low as 3° F. Meteorologists estimate it was the coldest winter the country had suffered since 1795.

OPPOSITE: The first woman cosmonaut, 26-year-old Russian Valentina Tereshkova, launched into space in *Vostok 6* on June 16, 1963: she spent almost three days in space, orbiting the earth 48 times. Although lacking experience and training by modern standards, her selection was influenced by her good proletarian credentials and her father's early death as a war hero.

1963

LEFT: Actress Liz Taylor sported a new look when she returned from the charity premiere of the film *Lawrence of Arabia* in Paris. Accompanying her on the trip was Welsh actor Richard Burton (opposite), although both Burton and Taylor were married to other people at this time. They met on the set of *Cleopatra* and began a legendary affair of their own. Subsequently they divorced their respective spouses and married each other for the first time in March 1964. The couple were renowned for their tempestuous relationship and married and divorced each other twice.

1963

OPPOSITE: Puppeteer Shari Lewis and show host Ed Sullivan pose with Lamb Chop and Topo Gigio. Topo Gigio was the lead character in a successful Italian puppet show that began in the 1950s. The coy, cute, and clever mouse traveled across the Atlantic to become a regular feature of *The Ed Sullivan Show*. The chemistry between Topo Gigio and Ed made the 10 inch mouse an international star.

RIGHT: Basil Brush was the creation of Peter Firmin, an English animator and artist who initiated many successful children's television series. A simply operated glove puppet, Basil, a fox, adopted the hearty style of an upper class Englishman with not very much intelligence and a preference for puns that were delivered suffixed with the expression "Boom Boom!". Basil Brush rose to fame as the familiar of TV magician David Nixon and eventually was given his own show.

1964

In August 1964 the Beach Boys were guests on *The Ed Sullivan Show*. They performed "I Get Around," just one of the 16 hit singles they released between 1962 and 1965, live in front of the studio audience. Pictured left to right: Brian Wilson, Mike Love. Ed Sullivan, Dennis Wilson, Al Jardine, and Carl Wilson. The Beach Boys appeared in their signature button-down collar striped shirts from the start of their career until 1966.

1964

OPPOSITE: Reverend Martin Luther King came to the fore of the civil rights movement in the US during the 1960s; he was one of the leaders of the 1963 March for Jobs and Freedom which assembled over 250,000 protesters in the National Mall in Washington to hear King give one of the most electrifying pieces of oratory in American history. "I have a dream" entered the English language in this unforgettable speech. He was assassinated in Memphis, Tennessee, in 1968, soon after urging his followers not to abandon the path of non-violent protest.

ABOVE: Malcolm X was a black activist with a more aggressive and separatist philosophy than King's. Having been brought up in very difficult conditions and imprisoned for petty crime, Malcolm X adopted the austere principals of the Nation of Islam while in jail. On his release he became one of the most influential African American leaders and thinkers. Not long before his assassination in 1965 he began to write his life story in collaboration with Alex Hayley, who would achieve fame for his novel *Roots. The Autobiography of Malcolm X* became a classic of both literature and political history.

ABOVE: The nuclear family at the heart of *Bewitched*, starring America's most beguiling TV witch, Samantha, played by Elizabeth Montgomery, whose talented nose could do pretty much anything with a twitch. Dick York played her slightly goofy but good-hearted husband Darrin. The show ran for eight seasons, with the first of 254 episodes screening in 1964.

OPPOSITE: Granada Television launched the gritty, northern soap opera *Coronation Street* across the ITV network in May of 1960, and despite the prevalence of kitchen-sink drama at the time, no one could have predicted that the series would still be running over 50 years later. Bernard Youens and Jean Alexander joined *Coronation Street* in June 1964 to play what was to become one of the show's favorite couples—Stan and Hilda Ogden.

1964

ABOVE: American sprinter Bob Hayes (center) about to win a qualifying heat for the 100 meters race at the 1964 Olympic Games. In the final he won the gold medal, running in adverse conditions yet matching the world record. His second gold came with the 4 x 100 meter relay, where a new world record was set. Going out on a high, Hayes left the track and field arena, joining football team Dallas Cowboys in the 1964 draft.

OPPOSITE: At the opening ceremony of the Tokyo Olympic Games in October 1964 Yoshinori Sakai, a student born in Hiroshima on the day the first atomic bomb devastated the city, carried the torch up the stairs to light the cauldron in the National Stadium: 5,151 athletes from 93 nations participated in the XVIIIth Olympiad.

1964

ABOVE: Irrepressible Freddie Garrity with the other members of the band Freddie and the Dreamers. The diminutive singer and frontman of the group was famous for his eccentric antics, jumping and bouncing around the stage with arms and legs flailing. Although the band were part of the Mersey sound that reverberated around the world in the wake of Beatlemania, all the band members were from Manchester.

OPPOSITE: Despite the massive explosion of British musical talent in the early 1960s, it was only the Rolling Stones who could challenge the Beatles' headline-grabbing abilities. The Stones infused pop music with a new creativity and rebelliousness fostered by their art school sensibilities, presenting a more "dangerous" and aggressive image on and offstage, epitomised by Jagger's strutting sexuality. Left to right: Charlie Watts, Keith Richards, Mick Jagger, Bill Wyman, and Brian Jones.

Pop singer Dusty Springfield checks out the latest in home fashion at the Ideal Home Exhibition in 1964. Born Mary Isabel Catherine O'Brien in London in 1939, Dusty aspired to become a singer from a very early age and in 1960 she joined forces with her brother Dion and Tim Field to form The Springfields. She embarked on her solo career in late 1963 and went on to phenomenal success during the 60s with hit singles "I Only Want to Be With You" and "You Don't Have to Say You Love Me." Dusty's distinctive, wide-ranging voice established her as one of the most notable white soul artists to make an impression in the US market.

Broad smiles greet this new piece of technology: the latest in domestic fan heaters. In the mid-60s a warm house in winter was a rarity: full central heating was a luxury for the wealthy and for the rest there might be only one heated room in the house. These ladies are looking forward to the instant heat afforded by the powerful output of this new device.

ABOVE: A brief break in filming on location of *The Ipcress File*, starring Michael Caine as Harry Palmer, the maverick secret service operative who is the antithesis of James Bond, pictured here with Sue Lloyd in the role of Jean Courtney. The movie was based on a novel by Len Deighton and won critical acclaim; it was followed over time by four sequels with Caine in the lead role, culminating in *Midnight in St. Petersburg* in 1996.

OPPOSITE: Newly married Peter Sellers and Britt Ekland. Sellers had been hired by director Billy Wilder to play opposite Dean Martin in *Kiss Me, Stupid* but six weeks into filming Sellers was struck down with a heart attack.

1964

ABOVE: Labour party leader Harold Wilson inspects posters in the press room of Transport House, the Labour party's HQ, in preparation for the election in October 1964. Labour were to win the election with a tiny majority of five seats. Wilson successfully gambled on calling a second election in March 1966, achieving a 98-seat majority, which gave a clear mandate to govern.

OPPOSITE: While the term Mod originally was originally applied to a small group of well-dressed existentialist London "jazz types," by 1964 the name was being applied to a youth sub-culture whose preferred mode of travel was a Vespa or Lambretta scooter. Smartly dressed under their pork pie hats and parkas, they regularly converged on British seaside towns and, perhaps having indulged in recreational drugs, would engage with their social rivals the Rockers, leading to street violence on an epic scale.

1964

ABOVE: Actress Shirley Eaton stars with Sean Connery in the third of the James Bond spy thrillers, *Goldfinger*, based on the novel by Ian Fleming. The movie, produced by Albert R. Broccoli and Harry Saltzman, was a huge critical and financial success and broke many box office records around the world. It won an Oscar for best effects and was the first Bond film to use a star (Shirley Bassey) to sing the theme tune. The iconic image of Eaton's gold-painted body used for promo material was a piece of marketing genius.

OPPOSITE: In his role as ladykiller, Bond enjoys encounters with limitless numbers of stunning-looking women. During the history of the franchise, few Bond girls have equalled the poise and grace of Honor Blackman, who plays Pussy Galore in *Goldfinger*. Blackman first came to fame as the leather-clad, crime-fighting Cathy Gale in the TV series *The Avengers*.

ABOVE AND OPPOSITE: When it was announced that Cassius Clay, later called Muhammad Ali, (opposite) would fight the powerful and experienced Sonny Liston (above) for the World Heavyweight title, few thought that Clay had any chance of winning. However, on February 25, 1964, Clay surprised everyone by surviving the first few rounds. By the end of round six Liston was beginning to tire, and when the bell rang to announce round seven Liston failed to answer.

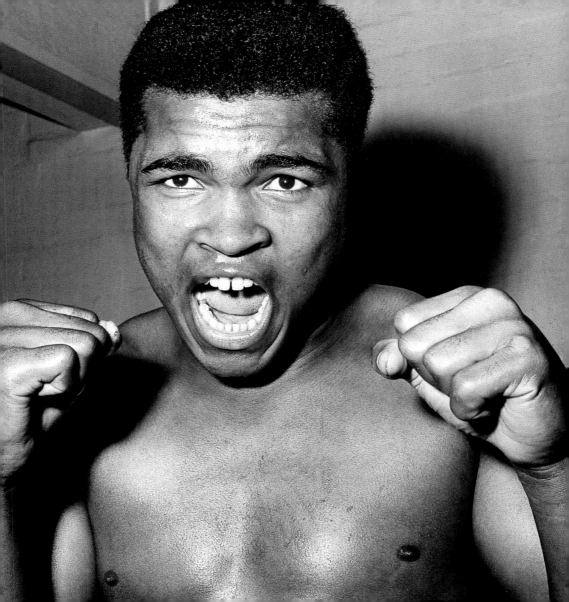

LEFT: Harold Sakata, the Hawaiian born actor who played Oddjob in the 1964 Bond movie *Goldfinger*. He carries his trademark weapon, the infamous steel-brimmed, sharpened bowler hat he spun through the air to attack enemies. Sakata was a former weightlifter and won a silver medal for the United States at the London Olympics in 1948.

OPPOSITE: Alfred Hitchcock offers some advice to to Sean Connery. After the success of the first two Bond movies, *Doctor No* and *From Russia With Love*, Sean Connery found himself much in demand. 1963 and 1964 were busy years for the rising star who, in addition to the Bond movies, also made *Woman of Straw* with Gina Lollobrigida and *Marnie* with director Alfred Hitchcock.

1964

OPPOSITE: President Lyndon B. Johnson and the first family captured by society photographer Fabian Bachrach. In November 1964 Johnson won a record landslide election victory against Republican nominee Barry Goldwater. That summer Johnson had passed the Civil Rights Act of 1964, which had been instigaged by JFK. Johnson's determination to implement the policies of his predecessor brought him widespread support but his efforts on the civil rights front lost votes in the South.

ABOVE: President Johnson's car is beseiged by crowds in Brooklyn during his campaign tour in New York. He is accompanied by Robert Kennedy, brother of assassinated president John F. Kennedy, who was campaigning to be elected as Senator for New York State.

ABOVE: Trainspotters at St. Pancras Railway Station in London. In May 1961 Dr Richard Beeching was appointed as the first Chairman of the British Railways Board to try to stem the losses the railway network was making as families and freight began the transition from rail to road. His solution was to produce a report two years later entitled "The Reshaping of British Railways," more commonly known as the Beeching Axe, which ultimately closed 3,000 stations and 4,000 miles of track.

OPPOSITE: Beeching relaxes in a mock-up of a new design for a first-class lounge on high-speed trains expected to be introduced by 1966. As well as reducing the rail network he introduced numerous modernizations, including the new British Rail logo he holds in this picture, which would replace the more traditional corporate identity in 1965.

ABOVE: The United Nations complex dominates this East River waterfront view of New York City with the Assembly Building a low-rise exception in the center. The high price of land in Manhattan forced buildings upward but strict architectural laws were introduced in the 1960s to ensure the quality of building continued the values of the Empire State and Chrysler Buildings, seen center and right in this 1964 photograph.

OPPOSITE: National Westminster Bank commissioned Architect Richard Sieffert to design their new headquarters building in the City of London in 1964. Their original specification was 450 feet but Sieffert's design pushed this up to 647 feet. Seen from above, the building took the shape of the NatWest logo. The site was occupied by two historic buildings and planning permission was not granted until 1970, with a compromise height of 600 feet rising through 43 floors. Building started in 1971 and took eight years to complete, providing London with a new iconic skyscraper that would remain its tallest building for 10 years.

Tailored suits were much worn in the 60s, with the shape becoming more box like. Jackets reached just below the waist with clearly defined buttons, and often a shift dress was worn underneath, Military-style double-breasted jackets were very popular and pillbox-type hats that complemented the outfit were designed to sit on the new geometric hairstyles.

1964

OPPOSITE: Legendary American singer Roy Orbison, whose country-based ballads were delivered with great vocal passion but with an impassive stage style. Orbison's early 1960s hits such as "Blue Bayou" gained him world renown and when touring top of the bill with the Beatles in 1963 the Fab Four were astonished by the audience reaction when Roy's low energy performance would gain him 14 encores.

RIGHT: One of the other distinctive male solo voices of the decade was Gene Pitney, pictured walking down Oxford Street on a visit to London in 1964. His best-known hit single, the Bacharach-David song "Twenty Four Hours From Tulsa," entered the UK charts in 1963, bringing him great popularity in Britain; on his visit he sat in on Rolling Stones recording sessions with Phil Spector, playing piano on some tracks. "Twenty Four Hours From Tulsa" was followed by three more hits in 1964, one of which was the Jagger/Richards composition "That Girl Belongs to Yesterday."

1964

ABOVE: Menzies Campbell takes the baton from fellow athlete Ron Jones during a training session. Before he opted for a career in politics, "Ming" was a successful sprinter who competed for the British team at the 1964 Summer Olympics in Tokyo.

OPPOSITE: John Surtees had already won seven motorcycling world titles when he made his Formula One debut in 1960. Going into the final race in 1964 fellow Briton Graham Hill led the table, but after Hill's car span off the track, Surtees clinched the title by just one point, becoming the only man to take world titles on both two wheels and four.

1964

LEFT: In swinging London there was no telling who you might find in the local bar. Here English fashion designer Mary Quant, left, enjoys a beer with her hairdresser Vidal Sassoon, who helped her create her trendsetting look. Sundra Mundy sits on the bar plucking a Hofner bass guitar similar to Paul McCartney's.

OPPOSITE: Russian dancer Rudolf Nureyev directing English prima ballerina Dame Margot Fonteyn (standing behind him) and members of the Royal Ballet corps in his new version of the ballet *Paquita*, which was staged in 1964. Nureyev, under growing threats from the KGB, had defected from Russia in 1961, while in Paris on tour with the Kirov Ballet. He was invited to join the Royal Ballet, where he and Fonteyn began their dance partnership. Fonteyn joined the Royal Ballet in her teens and remained with the company until she retired, just before her 60th birthday.

1964

In February 1964 Richard Petty achieved his first superspeedway win at the 1964 Daytona 500, leading the race for 184 of the 200 laps. Chrysler's potent new Hemi engine secured the Plymouth's manufacturer the top three finishing positions. Petty would go on to win a further six Daytona 500s and also seven NASCAR championships during his distinguished career, which earned him the nickname "The King."

1964

ABOVE: At 24 years old, American soul singer Dionne Warwick was becoming a worldwide sensation with her distinctive voice and classic songs provided by the Burt Bacharach and Hal David writing team. Her 1964 single, "Walk on By," set a standard not easily surpassed.

OPPOSITE: English actress Barbara Windsor puts on lipstick in her dressing room in August 1964. Six weeks later she was starring in the Broadway production of *Oh! What a Lovely War* following its surprise success in London's West End. She was nominated in the 1965 Tony Awards for her performance in the piece.

1965

Military pallbearers carry Sir Winston Churchill's coffin down the steps of St. Paul's Cathedral. When the former British Prime Minister died at the age of 90, the Queen decreed that a full state funeral should be held. Churchill's coffin was borne on a gun carriage through the West End of London to St. Paul's Cathedral. After the memorial service the coffin was escorted down the River Thames to Waterloo Station, where the funeral cortège continued its journey by train, eventually reaching St. Martin's Church in Bladon, near Oxford, where Churchill was buried in the family plot. His death elicited a massive response from the public. Over 300,000 mourners filed past the catafalque as he lay in state in Westminster Hall. On the day of the funeral thousands lined the streets and rail tracks to pay their respects while millions at home and abroad watched the events on television.

1965

OPPOSITE: The Moody Blues, original lineup: Graeme Edge, Denny Laine, Mike Pinder, Ray Thomas, and Clint Warwick. The English band from Birmingham had their first hit single with "Go Now" which released in 1964 but made number one on the singles chart in January 1965. The Moody Blues' distinctive sound and greatest success developed after the departure of Denny Laine and the arrival of replacement Justin Hayward in 1966.

RIGHT: Like The Beatles, Liverpool band The Searchers had a residency contract with the Star Club in Hamburg in 1962. Between 1963 and 1964 they had three number one hits, including "Needles and Pins." Unlike many of their contemporaries, they kept their performing career going with regular touring right up to the present day.

OPPOSITE: Easter 1965, and Mods on Brighton beach are watched over by police. Previous Easter Bank Holidays had seen vandalism and violence in Clacton and Margate as Mods clashed with Rockers, or "Greasers" who rode powerful motorcycles, wore black leather, and were a throwback to biker gangs represented in such films of the 1950s as *The Wild One*.

ABOVE: Ian Smith, Premier of Rhodesia, failed to get the agreement he sought with the British government and one month later, on November 11, he and his cabinet signed a Unilateral Declaration of Independence from Britain, which was to last until 1980 when the colony finally gained true independence with majority rule, changing its name from Rhodesia, named after colonist Cecil Rhodes, to Zimbabwe, after the ancient African city.

1965

LEFT: After a brief spell training as a set designer, Judi Dench began her acting career in amateur productions before her debut as a professional with the Old Vic Theatre Company. Most of her early work was in the theater, and she became known as one of the UK's finest Shakespearean actors. Her film career started slowly with a few minor roles in her early career. She became known to an international audience in the 1990s after taking over the role of M in the James Bond film *Goldeneye*, and received critical acclaim for her portrayal of Queen Victoria in *Mrs. Brown*.

OPPOSITE: In 1961 Diana Ross, Mary Wilson, and Florence Ballard, part of a vocal group called The Primettes, were signed to Detroit's premier record company, Motown Records, and renamed as The Supremes. By the mid-60s, they were Motown's most successful act. Through the early 1960s lead vocals were shared but gradually the record company focused on Diana Ross as lead on their singles releases; this culminated in Berry Gordy, head of Motown Records, renaming the act Diana Ross and the Supremes in 1967. In 1965 The Supremes released five albums and seven singles, including "Stop! In the Name of Love."

Moors Murderer Ian Brady pictured arriving at court where he was charged with the murders of three victims aged 10, 12, and 17, aided by Myra Hindley, who was dubbed "the most evil woman in Britain." The pair were called the Moors Murderers because most of their victims were killed on Saddleworth Moor, near Manchester. Initially the authorities held Brady and Hindley responsible for only three murders but they later confessed to two further crimes. Hindley's brother-in-law, David Smith, who witnessed the fifth and final murder—that of Edward Evans—and afterwards went to the police, said Brady killed with little emotion, as a butcher would do when carving a carcass.

The three Kray brothers, Reggie, Charles, and Ronnie, clasp hands in solidarity. Although notorious gang leaders in London's East End, the sharply dressed Krays behaved like aristocracy and mingled with all levels of society, thanks to the nightclub they owned in the West End. Finally convicted of murder in 1968, they began life sentences in prison. One twin, Ronnie, died in jail in 1995 and the other, Reggie, was released on compassionate grounds in 2000 to die a few weeks later from cancer; older brother Charles died in jail the same year while serving time for smuggling cocaine.

ABOVE: First broadcast in 1958, *The Black and White Minstrel Show* was a popular British TV program which attracted large audiences throughout the 1960s. The male singers were made up with black faces and adopted a mannered style of singing to give an overall parody of a music hall convention. Like many other aspects of life in the 1960s, this entertainment style was a continuation from a previous era, but as racial stereotyping became socially unacceptable the show was taken off BBC TV in the 1970s.

OPPOSITE: Members of the cast of puppet action show *Thunderbirds*, which drew a young audience to TV screens in 1965. Gerry Anderson and his wife Sylvia had a history of futuristic/fantasy puppet shows made for TV and developed their trademark "Supermarionation" style with plenty of tricky situations, explosions, and gadgets. The characterization of *Thunderbirds* was the best yet and in addition to the crew of International Rescue's five craft there was the ice-cool fashion icon Lady Penelope and her butler Parker who drives her pink six-wheel amphibious Rolls-Royce. The countdown start of the show became etched on the memory of the 60s generation: "5; 4; 3; 2; 1; Thunderbirds Are Go!"

1965

Apart from their success with albums such as *Beatles for Sale*, *Help!*, and *Rubber Soul*, in 1965 The Beatles were also celebrating the fact that John, aged 24, had learned to drive.

192

1965

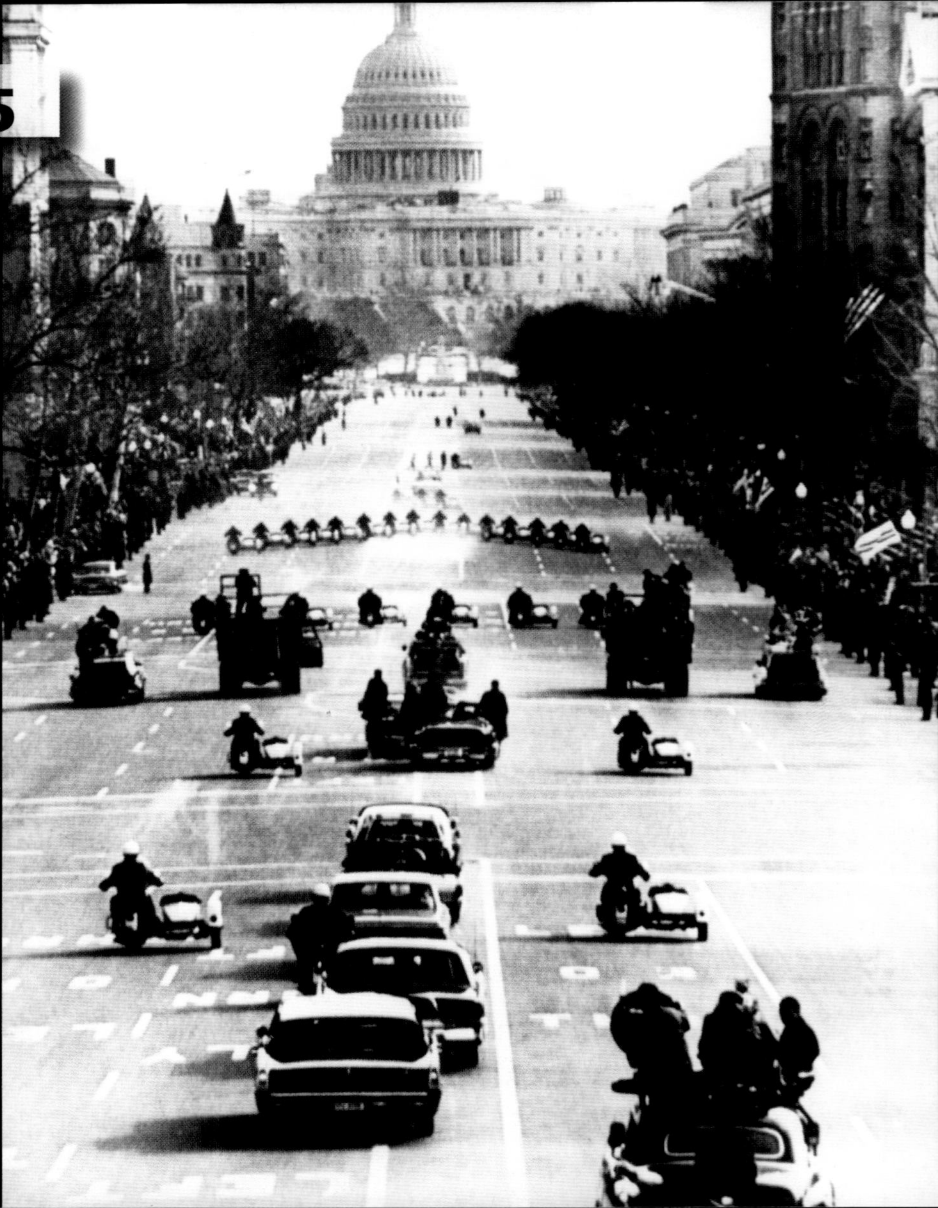

ABOVE: Lyndon B. Johnson takes his Oath of Office as the 36th President of the United States with Chief Justice Earl Warren at the Capitol. Ladybird Johnson focuses on her husband's words while Vice-President Hubert Humphrey looks on.

OPPOSITE: The presidential motorcade rolls down Pennsylvania Avenue en route from the White House to the Capitol building. Before his inaugural address, Johnson repeated the sentiments he expressed in Dallas on November 22, 1963, when President John F. Kennedy was assassinated: "I repeat now what I said on that sorrowful day, I will lead as best I can."

1965

RIGHT: Jane Fonda pictured with husband Roger Vadim in 1965, the year she starred in the spoof western *Cat Ballou*. Two comedies followed, including the 1967 *Barefoot in the Park*, co-starring Robert Redford. By the end of the decade Fonda had became interested in more serious projects and took on the role of Gloria Beatty in director Sydney Pollack's film *They Shoot Horses Don't They?*

OPPOSITE: Robert Redford with his wife and children in Munich, Germany, with Michael Connors and his wife. The two actors were taking a break from filming Gottfried Reinhardt's comedy movie *Situation Hopeless But Not Serious*, which also starred Alec Guinness.

1965

LEFT: A policeman carries a young woman protester down the steps of the Capitol in Washington, DC. The woman was among a group of civil rights demonstrators who staged a sit-in at the Capitol. Despite the civil rights legislation being enacted by the Johnson administration, resentment smoldered across the USA. In March a peaceful demonstration in Selma, Alabama, was brutally repressed by the infamous Sheriff Jim Clark. Like a bush fire, the authorities faced outbreaks of protest which climaxed in the Watts riots that rocked Los Angeles for six days in August. The Voting Rights Act of 1965 was signed by LBJ in the summer and within months, 250,000 new black voters had registered. The tide of democracy was on the turn.

OPPOSITE: A New York City policeman holds a youthful demonstrator against a car as he applies handcuffs after a civil rights demonstration flared into violence. The demonstrators were picketing the city's Board of Education building. The prospects for young African Americans were generally poor but in the ghetto environment of America's major cities such as Chicago, Los Angeles, and Washington DC, they were virtually hopeless with high unemployment, drugs, and crime generating despair in these depressed communities.

1965

ABOVE: Pop stars Cilla Black, Petula Clark, and Sandie Shaw. All three had successful singles. "Downtown" by Petula Clark reached number one in Britain and also topped the *Billboard* Hot 100 in the United States, making her the first British female artist to achieve this. Sandie Shaw's "Always Something There to Remind Me" sat at the top of the UK charts for three weeks and Cilla's "You're My World" spent five weeks a number one.

OPPOSITE: The Dave Clark Five pictured in 1965, when their hit "Over and Over" reached the top of the US charts. The band was named after the drummer Dave Clark, who employed the other band members and held all the copyright to their recordings. Between 1964 and 1967 the group from North London had 12 hits in the British top 40 and 17 records in *Billboard*'s top 40 in the States. They were very popular with American fans—having a "cleaner" image than the Beatles—and made a total of 18 appearances on *The Ed Sullivan Show*.

ABOVE: President Johnson and Vice-President Hubert Humphrey during a briefing on the progress of the Untied States space program at NASA. Dr. Homer Newell, Associate Administrator for Space Science and Applications, is demonstrating how the *Surveyor* soft landing moon probe would land on the lunar surface. *Surveyor 1* touched down successfully on June 2, 1966.

OPPOSITE: Computers were making great strides at the beginning of the electronic era but the technology was confined to enormous batch program operated machines based on electro-magnetic systems—transistors were in production but the silicon chip was still in development. An IBM machine occupied a large room and was run by programers who worked 24 hours a day loading their data via punch cards.

1965

Having seized power in 1959, Fidel Castro set about turning Cuba into a single party socialist state, declaring himself First Secretary of the Communist party in 1965. From his early days in power, the USSR increased its shadowy presence through rising numbers of "military advisors" and the provision of armaments that led to the 1961 Bay of Pigs invasion and then the Cuban Missile Crisis in 1962, bringing confrontation between the USA, Cuba, and Soviet Russia. Cuba's alliance with the Soviet Union endured throughout the Cold War, winning Castro the Order of Lenin and the status of Hero of the Soviet Union. Leonid Brezhnev came to power in 1964 and

State of Massachusetts Senator Edward Kennedy chats with President Johnson at the White House. This was Kennedy's first visit to the White House since his return to Washington following a near-fatal plane crash in June 1964. The pilot of the small private plane died, along with one of Kennedy's aides.

Nigel Lawson pictured in 1965 with first wife Vanessa and his first two daughters. Nigella (right) is now a celebrated cookery writer and presenter of her own TV cookery program. At the time of this photograph Lawson was City Editor of the *Daily Telegraph*. In 1974, after a successful career in journalism, Lawson became a Conservative Member of Parliament. In Margaret Thatcher's government he was appointed Chancellor of the Exchequer and was instrumental in reducing income tax and initiating Thatcher's privatization policy—selling off state-owned companies such as British Airways and British Gas.

Racing driver Graham Hill relaxes with two of his three children, including his son Damon, who was to follow his father into the sport and become Formula One World Champion in 1996. Graham Hill twice won the World Championship, in 1962 and 1968, and in 1966 was winner of the Indy 500, the first rooky winner since 1927. In 1969 he broke both his legs at the US Grand Prix and although he recovered, he was never able to repeat his success. Hill and five members of his racing team were killed in 1975 when the plane Hill was piloting crashed.

1965

RIGHT: An article in the women's section of a national newspaper reviewed a three-piece West of England check worsted suit. Traditional designs such as these were still much in vogue but gradually the newer synthetic materials and the simple, geometric Mary Quant dresses and mini skirts were beginning to dominate the fashion world.

OPPOSITE: Models wearing Triumph International Show swimsuits went on parade in 1965. New stretch fabrics such as nylon and Lycra were regularly being used and swimsuits often had cut-out sections or mesh net panels in the sides. Swimming hats were frequently decorated with colorful flower shapes.

1965

ABOVE: Actor and entertainer Roy Castle and Jennie Linden at Shepperton Studios during the making of the film *Dr. Who and the Daleks*, released in 1965 and based on the second *Dr. Who* TV series that had starred William Hartnell. In the movie the Doctor was played by Peter Cushing. It was the first Dr. Who story to be made in color; the television series continued to be screened in black and white for four more years.

OPPOSITE: In 1965 Hollywood actor Charlton Heston had just finished filming *The Agony and the Ecstasy*, in the role of Michelangelo, a movie that received five Oscar nominations. Heston's most celebrated film roles included Moses in *The Ten Commandments* and Rodrigo in *El Cid*. The 1959 epic adventure *Ben-Hur* earned him an Oscar for Best Actor with the film also receiving a further ten Oscars, including Best Picture.

1965

ABOVE: US Army helicopters fall into tight landing formation near Phouc Vinh in war zone "D," Vietnam. At the end of the Kennedy administration, the US had around 16,000 troops in Vietnam; by the end of 1965 President Johnson had increased that number to 184,000. Initially the US avoided initiating ground warfare, favoring its "Rolling Thunder" bombing campaign against the Vietcong, but in June LBJ authorized General William Westmoreland to engage in ground combat. The delivery of troops to the combat zone made the UH-1 Bell helicopter an icon of warfare; its initial designation in trials was HU-1, thus the nickname "Huey."

OPPOSITE: The body of a slain comrade is carried to an evacuation helicopter by soldiers of the US 1st Cavalry Division in the Ia Drang Valley early in November 1965. The escalation of US involvement in Vietnam was part of the ideology of LBJ's administration; although Congress voted funding, the American people were not consulted and the state of war was not publicized. Troop casualties during 1965 climbed to 1,500 dead and 6,000 wounded. Even a professional army would find such losses hard to justify, but conscription of civilians made such statistics unacceptable to many Americans, especially those eligible for the draft.

ABOVE: Celebrity photographer David Bailey married actress Catherine Deneuve in August 1965. Bailey and Deneuve were major artists of their generation and in big demand; in 1965 alone, Deneuve appeared in four movies. By 1972 the marriage had ended in divorce, though they remained friends. The same year as their separation, Deneuve had a daughter, Chiara, by actor Marcello Mastroianni; Bailey went on to marry model Marie Helvin three years later.

OPPOSITE: Hysteria awaits as The Beatles return from their European tour in July 1965, after 15 performances in France, Italy, and Spain. The Fab Four had recently completed their second film, '*Help!*', and just been awarded MBEs in the Queen's birthday honors list. Their latest single, "Ticket to Ride," topped the charts in Britain and the US.

1965

世界人民团结起予

ABOVE: China's second National Games, held in Beijing in 1965. Conceived in 1959, the games are the main sporting event in China, giving athletes the opportunity to compete at a national level. Nearly 6,000 athletes took part in the 18-day spectacle, with 130 national and nine international records broken. Many new young and talented athletes emerged at the games; China's economy was improving after three years of difficulties and sport had surged in popularity.

OPPOSITE: Liverpool captain Ron Yeats holds the FA Cup aloft as Bill Shankly salutes the crowd. As the open-topped bus toured the city, fans went wild with delight. The FA Cup had always proved elusive and it was the first time in the club's history that they had brought home the trophy. Since then they have won the title on six further occasions.

1965

March 21, 1965: Martin Luther King and fellow civil rights supporters arrive in Montgomery, Alabama, at the end of a five day, 54 mile walk to protest against the voting laws. On reaching Montgomery, King stood on the steps of the state capitol and delivered a speech that has become known as "How Long, Not Long."

1965

RIGHT: Australian folk group The Seekers topped the US and UK charts in February 1965 with their single "I'll Never Find Another You." Composed by Tom Springfield, the song made lead singer Judith Durham's voice a classic of the 1960s and The Seekers' homely image, combined with their tuneful songs, attracted audiences of all ages.

OPPOSITE: Bob Dylan in spring of 1965. Dylan's ballads with their social commentary made him the contemporary mouthpiece for the protest generation. He had hits with his own songs but they also provided success for other artists, such as The Byrds with "Mr. Tambourine Man," which topped the charts on both sides of the Atlantic in summer 1965. Dylan avoided stereotyping himself and, alongside his new album *Bringing It All Back Home*, Dylan went electric, causing some ire among his folk following.

1965

ABOVE: Queen Elizabeth greets Jacqueline Kennedy with her children, John Jr. and Caroline, and her brother-in-law Robert Kennedy during a poignant ceremony to unveil a monument to assassinated President John F. Kennedy at Runnymede, west of London. The stone tablet memorial, engraved with words from JFK's inaugural speech, is sited in an acre of land given to the United States by the people of Britain.

OPPOSITE: Jomo Kenyatta (left), who had become the first President of Kenya in 1964, talking with Ghanaian President Kwame Nkrumah at the third Commonwealth Prime Ministers' Conference at Marlborough House in London. Both African leaders had moved from the office of Prime Minister under British rule to President on gaining independence. Nkrumah's rule was cut short by a military coup in 1966, but Kenyatta would remain President of Kenya until his death in 1978 at the age of 83.

65

RIGHT: George Cukor's movie *My Fair Lady* enjoyed a long run in theaters and was an instant classic; production values were high and the movie's substantial budget was necessary to acquire the film rights, and employ Audrey Hepburn and other high profile contributors such as photographer Cecil Beaton, who took on the art direction. Accolades for the movie (and the soundtrack, which was a best-selling LP) fully justified Warner Brothers' confidence.

OPPOSITE: A radiant Audrey Hepburn. She was one of the first few artists to be paid a million dollars to play a role in a movie—in this case, Eliza Doolittle. At the 1965 Academy Awards *My Fair Lady* swept the board, taking eight Oscars with four further nominations.

1966

Left-handed pitcher Sandy Koufax, number 32, of the Los Angeles Dodgers pitching to Willie Mays, number 24, of the San Francisco Giants on May 5, 1966, in San Francisco, California. Koufax, three times winner of the Cy Young award, was forced to retire in 1966 because of severe arthritis in his elbow..

1966

OPPOSITE: A prototype of Concorde, the world's first and finest supersonic airliner. Concorde was the product of collaboration between the British Aircraft Corporation and French company Aerospatiale backed by their respective governments' funding. Work began on two prototypes in 1965 and the aircraft made its maiden flight in 1969, its sleek engineering looking decades ahead of its time. Here, Prince Philip, a keen pilot, gets a preview early in the planning stage.

RIGHT: Singer Sandie Shaw celebrates the news that she has been selected to represent Britain in the 1966 Eurovision TV song contest in Vienna. The 18-year-old singer from Essex, discovered by pop star Adam Faith, was often referred to as the "barefoot pop princess from the 1960s" and topped the British charts three times during the decade. She became the first UK act to win Eurovision with her performance of "Puppet on a String," a composition chosen by the British public. It reached the top of the charts and earned her a gold disk.

ABOVE: Mary Quant set the ball rolling in 1963 with her new, youthful style but by 1966 Carnaby Street, in London's Soho district, had become the center of a world fashion revolution and an essential stage in any tour of swinging London.

OPPOSITE: Twenty-year-old Sonia Ross is crowned Miss Britain 1966. Pictured with her are runners-up Nanette Slack (left) and Maureen Lidgard-Brown.

1966

LEFT: India's first and only woman Prime Minister Indira Gandhi chats with American President Lyndon Johnson before a dinner at the White House in Washington during a three-day official visit to United States, March 30, 1966. Gandhi was elected to power in January 1966; descended from a prominent political family, her father Jawaharlal Nehru was India's first Prime Minister and during his period of office Indira, by then married to Feroze Gandhi, acted as personal assistant to her father.

OPPOSITE: Sudanese rebels in training. Sudan gained independence from Great Britain in 1956 but the religious and cultural differences between the north and the south divided the nation. After independence the country was run largely by the Islamic north, which led to army officers from the south, who were predominantly Christian, setting up the Anya-Nya guerrilla movement. A civil war raged as the rebels in the south attempted to set up an independent state, successfully acquiring arms and support from other countries including Israel and the Soviet Union. The war resulted in the deaths of over 500,000 people and was only resolved in 1972 when the Addis Ababa Agreement granted the south autonomy from the north.

1966

LEFT: As well as hosting the World Cup finals in 1966, England reached the final of the competition, beating West Germany at Wembley by four goals to two after extra time. Here Jimmy Greaves, injured during the earlier rounds, puts his arm around an exhausted Alan Ball, who had played his heart out during the game.

LEFT: England captain Bobby Moore, surrounded by his team, kisses the Jules Rimet trophy.

ABOVE: Eusébio, the Portuguese footballer who was born in Mozambique, receives treatment for a cut eye in the match between Portugal and Hungary in the 1966 World Cup, played at Old Trafford. Eusébio, nicknamed "The Black Panther," played for Benfica for 15 years, making over 300 appearances and scoring 317 goals. He appeared for the national side on 64 occasions, netting a total of 41 goals and was named European Footballer of the Year in 1965.

ABOVE: A groundsman clears up empty beer bottles after a match at Anfield, the home of Liverpool Football Club.

1966

OPPOSITE: The cast of *Till Death Us Do Part* (from which CBS's long-running show *All in the Family* was derived) rehearse for the Christmas 1966 broadcast (left to right): Anthony Booth, as son-in-law Mike, Una Stubbs as daughter Rita, Dandy Nichols as Else, and Warren Mitchell as Alf Garnett. Although a comedy, the program hightlighted the bigotry and small-mindedness in its main character, Alf, a working class Conservative with volatile behavior and colorful language. Despite the increasingly liberal views of the time it was perhaps telling that for many the program caused more offense through Alf Garnett's coarse language than through the character's explicitly racist views.

RIGHT: Girls play the new craze game—"elastics" or Chinese rope.

ABOVE: A model shows off the latest wigs at Birmingham's Ideal Home Exhibition. The elaborate hairstyles of the early 1960s had been replaced by bobs and pageboy cuts.

OPPOSITE: Strong colors and a simple shapes were the hallmarks of many 60s designs.

1966

American golfer Billy Casper, who won the 1966 US Open at the Olympic Club, San Francisco, lines up a putt. Casper won 27 tournaments on the PGA Tour between 1964 and 1970 and was PGA player of the year in 1966. His putting skills were rated as the best of his era.

1966

RIGHT: Raquel Welch's statuesque features, well supported by her fur bikini, were put to good use in Hammer Studio's *One Million Years BC,* released in December 1966. Acting in this role was of secondary importance! Welsh's name was synonymous with "sex symbol" in the 1960s and 1970s.

OPPOSITE: Braybrook Street, in the shadow of Wormwood Scrubs prison, London, was the scene of the notorious shooting of three police officers. The unmarked police car stands where it stalled, beside the body of one policeman, behind it to the right, covered over, is another body. The third victim was at the wheel of the car when he was killed. All the officers were shot at point-blank range when they approached a suspicious van, which turned out to be occupied by three armed robbers.

Vietcong guerrilla suspects, blindfolded and linked arm to shoulder, are led by
US infantrymen to a central interrogation point near Long Thanh. The conflicts in
Southeast Asia marked a transition from conventional warfare to modern techniques
that involved terror and psychological tactics.

President Johnson walks along a White House corridor en route to address the nation over concerns about the resumption of bombing in North Vietnam. He is accompanied by Bill Moyers, Press Secretary, and George Bundy, Presidential Assistant. Bill Moyers would continue to be a significant figure in US society as a broadcaster, journalist, and commentator until the present day.

1966

LEFT: American cookery guru Julia Child tastes a dish. Child married her francophile husband in 1946 and when he was posted to Paris she began a lifelong relationship with French cuisine that turned her into a legend in the USA. In Paris she took cookery lessons, then started a school for American residents in her own kitchen with a couple of French women. They collaborated with Childs in Paris then back in New England as she wrote her classic *Mastering the Art of French Cooking,* published by Alfred Knopf in 1961, which became a cookery bible. However, Child's reputation was sealed by her TV series which began in 1963 and ran for 10 years.

OPPOSITE: Fanny Cradock, best known as the TV cook who partnered with hen-pecked husband Johnnie. As this picture shows, Fanny had authentic English eccentricity! Although not a trained cook, she had broad experience as a restaurant critic and was a tonic to a nation just emerging from the grip of postwar austerity, with her no-nonsense approach and her practical recipes that could be dressed up as something special.

1966

ABOVE: The cast of TVs' *Dixon of Dock Green*. Jack Warner (right) played Constable George Dixon. The long-running series was set in an East End of London police station; it began in 1955 and ended in 1976, during which time British society was transformed. The program format was little more than a domestic drama, with George Dixon in a fatherly role giving a short homily while standing outside the station under the blue police lamp. Although popular with the British public, the influence of racy police drama from the USA gave the audience an appetite for more action, leading to the police drama *Z-Cars*.

OPPOSITE: One of the best known and loved double acts of television history, Eric Morecambe and Ernie Wise rehearse for their latest television series. Their shows were typified by good, clean, family entertainment and were popular right up until Eric's death from a heart attack in 1984. The guest list was like reading a section of the *Who's Who* directory, and stars of stage and screen lined up to appear on the show and allow themselves to be parodied, mocked, and insulted.

BOWERY

BARI PIZ

ABOVE: The Bowery sits adjacent to New York City's Lower East Side and in the 1960s was the city's "Skid Row." The street that gives the area its name is one of New York's oldest thoroughfares, derived from the Dutch word for farm, given by Peter Stuyvesant to the track between Fort Amsterdam and his homestead. As a low-rent area it provided housing for impoverished artists and thinkers. In 1966 the founder of the Hare Krishna movement, A. C. Bhaktivedanta Swami Prabhupada, lived here, as did artist Cy Twombly. The gentrification of the area began in the 1990s and the story today is very different.

OPPOSITE: US President Lyndon B. Johnson receives a tickertape welcome in Sydney, Australia, at the start of his three-day visit, part of a 17-day tour of Pacific and Asian countries. This was the first visit of a US president to Australia and although Johnson was on his way to a regional summit in the Philippines, his visit was seen as a smart political move to encourage Australias' continuing support in the Vietnam conflict. Australia had a military presence in Vietnam from 1962 and steadily increased its commitment until over 7,000 troops were engaged. Robert Menzies' Australian government also introduced conscription to support the war effort—the reason being the threat to Australia from communism spreading from Southeast Asia.

ABOVE: In the 1960s, the US and Soviet space programs hotted up the fascination for space travel and extra-terrestrial beings. The general consensus was that aliens traveled in flying saucers and the occupants of Mars were little green men, a viewpoint that was challenged by US comedy TV series *My Favorite Martian*, where stranded Alien "Uncle Martin" looks pretty human. The popular series ended in 1966 but the epic *Star Trek* began the same year to "boldly go" around the universe where extraterrestrials like these hominids would be nothing compared to Captain Kirk's problems—especially when these studio characters could be so easily distracted by nearby celestial bodies.

OPPOSITE: Through the early 1960s Ike and Tina Turner became hugely popular as a live act, continuously touring and performing around the USA. Tina's voice and the backing sound of the Ikettes along with music that really rocked was an unbeatable combination put together by Ike, leader of the roadshow. However Tina would reveal later that Ike was a domineering bully with a drug problem and even though recording success came to them with the 1966 hit "River Deep, Mountain High," Tina would pursue a solo career and divorce Ike in the mid-70s.

1966

OPPOSITE: This scene is not a celebration of domestic harmony: the household is concentrating on a live boxing match—a development of new satellite technology heralded by the launch of Earlybird in 1965. Sports promoters now had access to unlimited global audiences and the rewards increased accordingly.

RIGHT: In 1966, Muhammad Ali successfully defended his World Heavyweight title three times in Toronto, London, and Houston, the last in November against Cleveland Williams, KO'd in the third round. Here he weighs in for his second fight with Britain's Henry Cooper; at their first meeting, 'Enry's 'Ammer knocked Clay to the canvas, earning Ali's enduring respect. In May 1966 Cooper didn't make it past the sixth round when he was knocked out by Ali.

1966

LEFT: Cilla Black, managed by Brian Espstein until his death in 1967, was rapidly carving out a career as an all-round entertainer. At the start of 1966 Cilla released the hit record "Alfie," the theme song from the movie of the same name, written by the Bacharach/David team and performed on the sound track by Cher. By the end of the decade her records had outsold all the other British female recording artists.

OPPOSITE: A mauve mini-pants suit with blue daisy print by Harbro. As the sixties moved on, hem lengths diminished, with 1969 known as the "year of the micro-mini."

1966

OPPOSITE: American evangelist Reverend Billy Graham preaching at one of his rallies. Billy Graham attracted enormous audiences to the stadiums and giant auditoriums he hired for what he called his Crusades, which he conducted around the world as well as in the USA. His straight-talking revivalism and neutrality in politics, combined with his relatively frugal earnings, gained him the respect of the American people—to the highest level. Lyndon Johnson valued his counsel and spent his last night in the White House in the company of Billy Graham; LBJ's successor, Richard Nixon, invited Graham to join him for his first evening in the White House. A strong supporter of the civil rights movement, Graham once put up bail for Martin Luther King.

RIGHT: Frantic rescue scenes at the Pantglas Junior School in Aberfan, Wales, after a giant spoil-tip from local coal-mining collapsed, engulfing the entire school in rubble and mud. Two thousand volunteers poured into the village to join attempts to rescue those trapped inside, but the final death toll eventually totaled 116 children and 28 adults.

66

ABOVE: Three of England's World Cup winning heroes and West Ham teammates (left to right): Geoff Hurst, who scored a hat trick in the final against West Germany, Bobby Moore, captain, and Martin Peters.

OPPOSITE: Salvatore Bono and Cherilyn Sarkisian, better known by their performing name, Sonny and Cher, met in 1962 in a coffee bar where Cher, aged 16, was working. Bono was employed in Phil Spector's studio doing backing vocals and got Cher involved. Eventually they started to perform together, achieving the smash hit "I Got You Babe" in 1965. The couple won massive TV and live audiences, not just because of their great songs but because they seemed to capture the carefree style of their generation, for whom Cher would be a lasting icon.

1966

LEFT: Pickles, the black and white mongrel dog who rose to fame after finding the Jules Rimet World Cup trophy. Four months before the 1966 World Cup competition, the trophy was on display in Westminster Central Hall, London, when it went missing one Sunday afternoon. Seven days later, while out walking with his owner David Corbett, Pickles unearthed the cup, wrapped in newspaper, under a garden hedge. After England won the trophy, Pickles was invited to the celebratory banquet and allowed to lick the plates, while his owner received a £6,000 reward.

OPPOSITE: Jack Nicklaus holds the claret jug, the British Open Golf Championship trophy, after taking the title at Muirfield, near Edinburgh, in 1966. At 26 he was the youngest player to win the championship. The American had turned professional five years earlier and had already won the Masters, the US Open, and the PGA Championship. His success at Muirfield meant that he had achieved a Career Grand Slam.

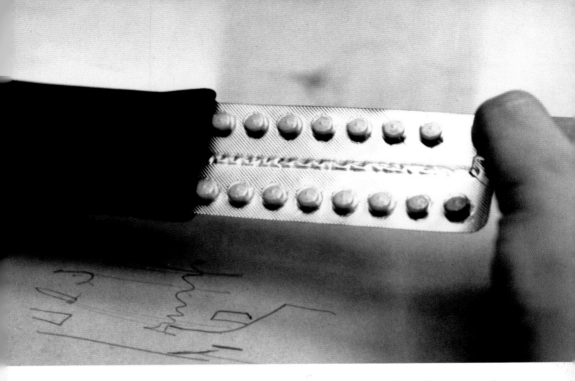

ABOVE: An important development of the 60s and a keystone of female liberation was the contraceptive pill. Much controversy surrounded "the Pill"—both from a medical perspective and because of the moral issues arising from the sexual freedom the pill facilitated. Although approved for medical use at the beginning of the 1960s, it was not available to all women through the USA until 1972. An FDA report published in 1966 found that there was no medical risk to women taking the pill, a standpoint that would later be overturned. Although the pill is most often associated with the sexual liberation of women, its main effect was to revolutionize the role of women in the professions, enabling them to compete in the male dominated workplace.

OPPOSITE: Sixties fashion progressed and took quantum leaps propeled by new fabrics, female liberation, and a more relaxed attitude to nudity and revealing parts of the body previously kept covered. Topless swimwear and dresses didn't catch on but cutaway dresses and the wonders of PVC led to new fashionwear that chimed with the swinging sixties.

1966

I AM KINKY RU 2? P.T.O

ABOVE: Robert Vaughn (right) and David McCallum find themselves in yet another tight spot in TV spy/ action series *The Man From U.N.C.L.E.* Since James Bond creator Ian Fleming was involved in the making of the show it's not surprising that all the ingredients of 007's world were drawn into the program—clever gadgets and cunning weaponry aided the battle against evil THRUSH whose object was, of course, world domination. The series was popular and won numerous awards, especially in the 1966 Emmys, Golden Globes, and even the Grammys. It ran for four seasons over 105 episodes, eventually launching spin-off *The Girl From U.N.C.L.E.*, starring Stefanie Powers.

OPPOSITE: North London band The Kinks, display some of their fun-loving antics which escalated to onstage violence in some of their performances. The band had already gained a name for themselves in 1964 with "You Really Got Me," which made it into the US charts as well as being number one in the UK. In 1966 "Sunny Afternoon" was the hit of the summer, its light social satire a natural sequel to "Dedicated Follower of Fashion" which topped the UK charts in February but only made it to 36 in the *Billboard* Hot 100.

Mario Andretti celebrates after winning the 1967 Daytona 500 in February 1967. Andretti first encountered racing when, as a child, he observed a stretch of the famous Mille Miglia in his native Italy. In America he started out in stock-car racing and went on to be one of motorsport's most versatile champions, still the only American driver to have won Formula One (1978) and the only driver ever to have career wins in all three of Formula One, Indianapolis 500 and Daytona 500.

OPPOSITE: Rolling Stones Keith Richards and Mick Jagger, along with gallery owner Robert Fraser, were charged with possession of cannabis and some legally prescribed amphetamines at Keith's Sussex home in February of 1967. Robert Fraser was found in possession of heroin. Jagger and Richards were found guilty of drug offenses at Chichester court, and given custodial sentences. They were bailed the following day, pending an appeal, which eventually cleared them. Fraser was given a six-month jail sentence, of which he served four months.

RIGHT: Mick Jagger's girlfriend Marianne Faithfull was another familiar face on the London music scene and was present at the drugs raid at Keith Richards' home. It was widely reported at the time that she was found wearing only a fur rug. Faithfull at this time was a cocaine addict and would end up living on the street for two years after her relationship with Jagger ended in 1970.

Arsenal center forward George Graham
marries model Marie Zia at Marylebone
Register Office in London. Terry Venables
(left) is best man, who despite playing for
rivals Tottenham Hotspur is a good friend
of the groom.

Pat Phoenix in her role as Elsie Tanner, the sex symbol of TV soap *Coronation Street*, marries second husband, GI Sergeant Steve Tanner, ensuring her character would be known for the rest of the series as Elsie Tanner. Playwright and director Jack Rosenthal directed this episode and allegedly had to coax Phoenix from her dressing room when she had a severe case of nerves about her "wedding day." Her marriage to Steve didn't last long—he was murdered not long after, with suspicion being thrown on various cast members.

1967

RIGHT: Warren Beatty, brother of movie star Shirley MacLaine, appeared in three pictures in addition to his role in *Lilith* in 1964, but it was not until 1967, with the release of *Bonnie and Clyde,* that he became well known, producing and starring in the film opposite Faye Dunaway.

OPPOSITE: US actor Clint Eastwood made a name for himself as the star of TV's *Rawhide*, where he also made his first forays into scriptwriting and direction, but it was the *A Fistful of Dollars* and its sequels, *For a Few Dollars More* (1966), and *The Good, the Bad and the Ugly* (1967), all of which were highly succesful at the box office, that brought him worldwide recognition.

Super Bowl I was the name given to the first ever Super Bowl game, between AFL champions Kansas City Chiefs and NFL champions Green Bay Packers. Pictured here are members of the Green Bay Packers offense, including Bart Starr (15), Jerry Kramer (64), Elijah Pitts (22), Forrest Gregg (75), Jim Taylor (31), Marv Fleming (81), and Max McGee (85), huddling up prior to a play during the match on January 15, 1967, at the Coliseum in Los Angeles, California. The Packers won 35 to 10, with Bart Starr picking up MVP (Most Valued Player). The two major leagues would merge in 1970 under the title NFL.

1967

LEFT: David Frost makes eye contact with *The Avengers* star, Diana Rigg. Rigg played Emma Peel, the second female lead in *The Avengers*, who had more edge than her predecessor Cathy Gale. Peel had her own agenda, was good in a tight corner, and looked stunning in her leather catsuit. David Frost followed his successful *That Was The Week That Was* with *The Frost Report*, which ran for 28 episodes over two seasons.

OPPOSITE: American comedy actor and entertainer Phil Silvers spent his early career working as a character actor in various film studios. His most famous role came to fruition in 1955 when he played Sergeant Bilko in *The Phil Silvers Show*. He returned to the big screen in the 1960s, appearing in *40 pounds of Trouble*, *It's A Mad, Mad, Mad, Mad World*, and *Follow That Camel*, from the Carry On series. Back in the television studio he also made 30 episodes of *The New Phil Silvers Show*.

LEFT: In 1967 Sidney Poitier starred in three successful movies: *To Sir, With Love, Guess Who's Coming to Dinner,* and *In the Heat of the Night* (left), in which he played the detective Virgil Tibbs. *In the Heat of the Night* was followed by two sequels—*They Call Me MISTER Tibbs! (1970)* and *The Organization (1971).*

OPPOSITE: Joan Collins was raised in a show business family and began performing at a young age, enjoying a long career in both film and television. Joan's younger sister, Jackie, also had her share of success in the 1960s, publishing her novels *The World is Full of Married Men* (1967) and *The Stud* (1969).

1967

OPPOSITE: The ravaging of Vietnam by immense bombing and napalm campaigns carried out by US forces and the evacuation of some 13 million people from rural areas achieved little military or political progress. By 1967 the war was becoming increasingly unpopular both in the US and abroad, giving rise to an international peace movement.

RIGHT: The anti-war movement was represented by many different factions; there was a peaceful element comprised of hippies and other alternative groups whose direct actions consisted of sometimes absurdist "Happenings" and street theater, such as placing flowers in soldiers' gun barrels at demonstrations, but there were also some radical left-wing factions condoning and encouraging anti-social and criminal behavior in order to disrupt the war effort and resist the perceived wider social evils of capitalism.

1967

OPPOSITE: Summer of 1967 became immortalized as "the Summer of Love," with San Francisco as its hub. In June 1967 The Beatles took the theme global, performing their specially composed song "All You Need Is Love" watched by 400 million people on the first worldwide satellite TV link-up. This would be their last live televised performance. Earlier in June they released their groundbreaking psychedelic album *Sgt. Pepper's Lonely Hearts Club Band,* which received four Grammy Awards and spent 175 weeks in the *Billboard* 200, 15 of them in the number one position.

RIGHT: Stevie Wonder, aged 17, had dropped the "Little" from his stage name and in 1967 released his classic album *I Was Made to Love Her,* whose title track, released as a single, was a major hit for his Tamla Motown record label.

ABOVE: An injured Israeli soldier is given water and medical attention during the Six-Day War. An Arab coalition led by President Nasser of Egypt took a series of steps in spring 1967 which Israel interpreted as a real military threat: on June 4, Israel launched a pre-emptive offensive that kept it at an advantage over the Egyptian, Syrian, Jordanian, and Iraqi forces that were engaged against it. Israeli casualties, at 983 killed and 4,517 wounded, were fewer than their pre-war estimates and considerably less than the estimated losses of the more numerous Arab coalition forces.

OPPOSITE: Israeli Prime Minister David Ben-Gurion (center), surrounded by soldiers, visits the Wailing Wall in Jerusalem on June 12, 1967, after Israeli troops captured the Old City in the Six-Day War. Crippling Arab air capability, Israel took the Sinai Peninsula in three days, moved the Jordanian and Syrian borders, and occupied the strategic Golan Heights. The Six-Day War ended on June 10, 1967.

ABOVE: In February 1967 Albert DeSalvo, known as The Boston Strangler, escaped from the psychiatric hospital in which he was serving a life sentence for the sexual assault and murder of 13 women in the Boston area. DeSalvo left a note on his bed saying his escape was to draw atttention to conditions in the hospital and he gave himself up to the police the next day in Lynn, Massachusetts.

OPPOSITE: Michael Abdul Malik, known as Michael X, the civil rights activist and Black Power leader, settled in Notting Hill, London, after leaving his native Trinidad and Tobago and made his living from drug pushing and pimping. In 1967 Malik was the first non-white person to be arrested under England's Race Relations Act after he actively encouraged shooting any black man seen with a white woman. Following an 18-month prison sentence he formed the Racial Adjustment Action Society (RAAS) and set up a commune in North London, known as the Black House. When Malik was arrested for extortion John Lennon stepped in and paid his bail. Michael X grasped the opportunity and fled back to Trinidad, where he began another commune; he was eventually arrested for murder in 1972 and hanged three years later.

By mid-1967 President Lyndon Johnson's popularity had evaporated: escalation of US involvement in Vietnam and the growth of inflation and taxes outweighed the social progress made by his administration. On top of this came renewed confrontation with Russia when the US Sixth Fleet took up position in the Eastern Mediterranean during the Six-Day War build-up, in readiness to protect Israel should Russia enter in support of Soviet ally Syria. Russian President Alexei Kosygin threatened war and sent a naval presence to shadow US and British vessels.

The Philharmonic Hall, New York, designed by Max Abramovitz, was the first auditorium to be opened in the Lincoln Center for the Performing Arts in 1962. Although it had to be extensively refurbished in the mid-70s to improve its acoustics, in 1967 it was one of New York City's leading music venues, home of the New York Philharmonic Orchestra and hosting sell-out concerts by Simon and Garfunkel, Mahalia Jackson, Janis Joplin, and Donovan to name a few. It became an elegant motion picture house for the 5th New York Film Festival in September 1967. It was renamed Avery Fisher Hall in 1973.

ABOVE: Vanessa Redgrave working with composer Monty Norman for the musical *Camelot*, released in 1967. Redgrave starred alongside Richard Harris; the film won three Academy Awards and two further nominations. Redgrave's highly successful acting career spans six decades, winning her many nominations and a single Academy Award, for Best Actress in a Supporting Role for her part in the movie *Julia*. Redgrave has also maintained her reputation as a prolific and unstinting political activist since the early 1960s.

OPPOSITE: Conductor Daniel Barenboim rehearses cello virtuoso Jacqueline du Pré; they began a relationship after meeting in 1966 and in June 1967, when the Six-Day War ended, they flew to Jerusalem where she immediately converted to Judaism and married Barenboim the next day at the Western Wall. The marriage was turbulent but their artistic partnership was magical. Du Pré died from multiple sclerosis in 1987. Barenboim's West-Eastern Divan Orchestra was founded in 1999, using music to improve understanding between young Jews and Arabs.

ABOVE: The vast set at Pinewood Studios for *You Only Live Twice*, the fifth film in the 007 spy series. Sean Connery again starred as James Bond but this was to be his penultimate appearance in the role. The screenplay was written by Roald Dahl and for the first time, only the characters from the original book were used and a totally new storyline was created. With Nancy Sinatra providing the theme music, the movie eventually grossed over $111 million worldwide.

OPPOSITE: Scenes during the filming of *Half a Sixpence* on the beach at Eastbourne. The British musical, directed by George Sidney and based on an H. G. Wells novel, was set in Edwardian England and starred Tommy Steele and Julia Foster in the main roles. Steele rose to fame as a rock and roll singer in the 1950s, performing cover versions of US hits. During the 60s he moved into stage and film musicals including *Finian's Rainbow* with Petula Clark and Fred Astaire.

ABOVE: Donald Campbell's goal was always to hold the world speed record on both land and water; he achieved his ambition in 1964 when he reached 276.33mph on water and 403.10mph on land at two locations in Australia. In January 1967 Campbell again attempted to break the water speed record using his boat the *Bluebird K7*, this time on Coniston Water in England's Lake District. However, toward the end of the measured mile the front of the boat lifted at 45 degrees, somersaulted, and nose-dived into the water. The hull sank and Campbell was killed instantly. The wreckage and Campbell's body remained in the lake until located by divers over 30 years later.

OPPOSITE: Francis Chichester sailed *Gypsy Moth IV* single-handed around the world in 226 days, setting out from Plymouth, England, in August 1966, returning in May 1967. He was the first solo yachtsman to achieve this feat, west to east via the great capes, and was knighted by Queen Elizabeth II, using the same sword that Queen Elizabeth I used to knight Sir Francis Drake.

1967

RIGHT: British tennis player Roger Taylor takes on Wilhelm Bungert during the 1967 Wimbledon semi-final, eventually losing the match 2 sets to 3. Taylor also reached the semi-final at Wimbledon in 1970 and 1973.

OPPOSITE: The hugely successful TV sitcom *Gilligan's Island*, first aired between 1964 and 1967, followed the adventures of seven castaways stranded on an island.

Dr. Christiaan Barnard performing an operation, Christiaan Barnard found fame when as a pioneering heart surgeon he performed the first successful heart transplant operation at the Groote Schuur Hospital in Cape Town in December 1967. Although the recipient only lived 18 days after the operation, his further transplants were more successful.

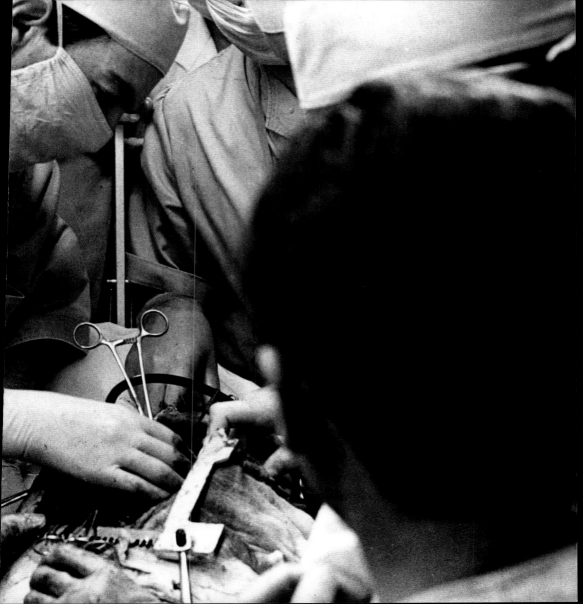

1967

OPPOSITE: England and Stoke City goalkeeper Gordon Banks keeps the ball out of the net in training.

ABOVE: Young Manchester United star George Best in action. Best was one of the greatest footballers of all time, but in this developing age of celebrity cultural icons, Best, sometimes nicknamed "the fifth Beatle," was equally well known for his other passions: womanizing and drinking.

BURIAL CHAMBER
ENT VILLAGE

ABOVE: On March 18, 1967, the supertanker *Torrey Canyon* ran aground off the coast of Cornwall, England. She was carrying a full cargo of 120,000 tons of crude oil. Plans to refloat the vessel failed and here people gather at Land's End to watch the bombing of the tanker, undertaken to speed the breaking up of the ship and the treatment of the vast spillage that devastated marine life in the area and polluted large areas of the Cornish and French coastlines. It was the first disaster on such a scale and the authorities were ill-prepared for the cleanup operation; as a consequence new international legislation was implemented which made clear the liabilities of the shipping companies carrying such dangerous cargo.

OPPOSITE: Student protests were a feature of the 1960s, here they stage a sit-in at the prestigious London School of Economics.

1967

ABOVE: The Pink Floyd lineup: (left to right): Rick Wright, Roger Waters, Syd Barrett, and Nick Mason. Formed in London in 1965, by 1967 they had landed a recording contract with EMI, appeared on *Top of the Pops* and toured with Jimi Hendrix. The following year Dave Gilmour joined the group to replace Syd Barrett, who had a serious drug problem. Their first album, *The Piper at the Gates of Dawn*, reached number six in the British charts but got no further than 131 in the *Billboard* 200. Although increasingly successful as the decade wore on, their classic albums *Dark Side of the Moon* and *Wish You Were Here* were not released until the mid-1970s.

OPPOSITE: Jimi Hendrix (center) made his name in the UK, when he formed The Jimi Hendrix Experience and appeared on TV shows *Ready, Steady, Go!* and *Top of the Pops* in 1966. His first album, *Are You Experienced?* reached the second spot in the British album charts. He finally achieved success in the States after appearing at the Monterey International Pop Festival, setting fire to his guitar in the final number and throwing the remaining pieces into the crowd. In September 1970 Hendrix was found dead in a London apartment and post-mortem results revealed that he had asphyxiated in his own vomit.

Young mods wait outside
the Tiles Club in London's
Soho, where many ska bands
performed. The banner
advertises Radio Luxembourg,
which, unlike the pirate stations
floating offshore, had a secure
European base and a license to
operate dating back to the 1920s.
Although BBC's new station
Radio 1 had become immediately
popular with its young audience,
Radio Luxembourg continued to
have a following.

OPPOSITE: Chevrolet's Impala, available in the 1965 series as hard top or convertible, was General Motors' best-selling model with over a million sold in the US. The original Impala began production in the late 1950s and was intended to offer "a prestige car within the reach of the average American citizen." The formula kept on working—as this picture shows.

ABOVE: In Britain, the MGB "Roadster" sports car was the car to be seen in, unless of course you had one of the new Mini Coopers! MG was Britain's most popular sporting marque, though Jaguar occupied the high end and the Triumph TR series were keen rivals. The MGB was a transitional design, innovative for its time and Britain's best-selling sports car, with production running from 1962 to 1980. Popular in the USA, the MGB underwent a number of design changes in 1968 (the Mk II) under the new British Leyland ownership and again in the MkIII that blurred its traditional lines but met the USA's increasingly rigorous safety requirements and emission laws.

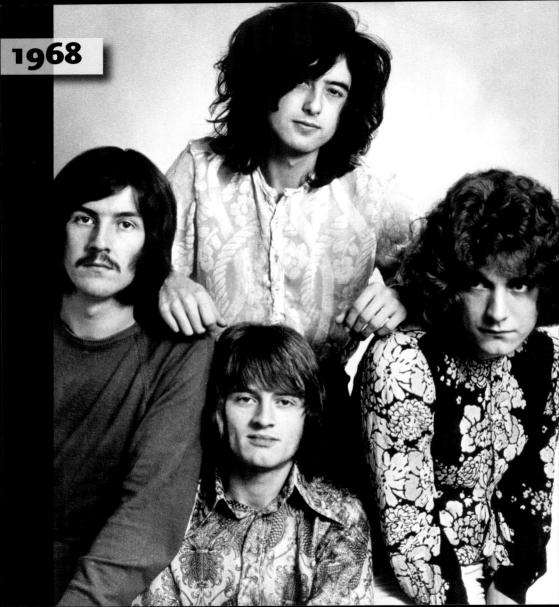

OPPOSITE: Led Zeppelin, pioneers of heavy metal rock (left to right: John Bonham, Jimmy Page (back), John Paul Jones, and Robert Plant), morphed out of The New Yardbirds to take the world by storm in 1968 with their new name, a play on the expression "lead balloon." Their signing to Atlantic Records in the USA for a record $200,000 was a sign of exuberance and excess to come. In their first 12 months as a band, Zeppelin released two best-selling albums and completed four US and UK concert tours.

RIGHT: Perhaps the first manufactured pop band, The Monkees proved a hit with teenage girls the world over. An unashamed copy of The Beatles, the band were created for a TV series, *The Monkees*, which would be a platform for their musical releases. The series ran from 1966 to 1968 and was a mix of sitcom, music, and offbeat humor. Studio executives were surprised by the success of the band's live tour through summer of 1967, their artistry proving more than just acting talent.

1968

LEFT: American athlete James "Jim" Hines won the gold medal for the 100 meters at the Mexico Olympic Games in a time of 9.95 seconds, not only setting a new world record but also becoming the first athlete to run the distance in under 10 seconds; a record that remained unbroken for another 15 years. He also helped his teammates win gold and set another world record in the 4 x 100 meters.

OPPOSITE: Bob Beamon shattered the world record for the long jump on October 18, clearing 29 feet, $2^1/_2$ inches, two feet longer than the existing record, which had been set by the man who coached him, Ralph Boston.

1968

ABOVE: American high jumper Dick Fosbury won gold at the 1968 Olympics. Fosbury's unique jumping style took advantage of the new foam landing beds which were replacing the sandpits that had required athletes to land on their feet, or at least land with care. His jumping style, landing on his back, entered sporting language as the "Fosbury Flop."

OPPOSITE: The winners' podium of the men's 200 meters race at the 1968 Olympics in Mexico City. Tommie Smith (center) took gold, setting a new world record; Australian Peter Norman took silver; and Smith's fellow American, John Carlos, bronze. The two African Americans used their position to make a political statement, raising the black-gloved Black Power salute. Peter Norman supported their viewpoint, joining the Americans in wearing an Olympic Project for Human Rights badge. All three athletes were censured for their standpoint, with the two Americans being ejected from the Games.

ABOVE: Lew Grade was one of the most successful television producers of the 1960s, commissioning programs such as *Sunday Night at the London Palladium*, *The Saint*, *The Prisoner*, *Emergency Ward Ten*, *Thunderbirds*, and *The Muppets*, and producing the *Pink Panther* movies.

OPPOSITE: Welsh folk singer Mary Hopkin was one of the first artists to sign up to The Beatles' Apple label after Twiggy had watched her performance on TV talent show, *Opportunity Knocks* and immediately contacted Paul McCartney. Her debut single "Those Were the Days," produced in 1968 by McCartney, shot to number one in Britain and number two in the *Billboard* Hot 100. Hopkin was selected to represent Britain in the 1970 Eurovision Song Contest with "Knock Knock, Who's There." The song took second place behind "All Kinds of Everything," performed by the Irish singer Dana.

1968

ABOVE: The interior of Hatchetts bar in Dover Street in Piccadilly, London. This coffee bar shows the increasing sophistication needed to meet the standard of swinging London—continental modernism, a zinc bar atmosphere, and some crazy montages made the late 60s coffee bar the cool place to hang out and drink Italian coffee.

OPPOSITE: Home fashion on display at the 1968 Ideal Home Exhibition. The Opus 22 range pictured here shows the influence of modernism in domestic furnishing—especially from Scandinavia.

1968

ABOVE: This mother is dressed in the height of fashion, with a mini length fun fur coat, and the baby sports the flag. The Union Flag or Union Jack was incorporated into all sorts of designs in the latter half of the 1960s as Britain became synonymous with cutting-edge fashion and style.

OPPOSITE: Top Radio 1 disk jockey Tony Blackburn, who launched the BBC's new radio station the previous year by playing The Move's "Flowers in the Rain," smiles for England! After leaving pirate station Radio London, Blackburn would remain with Radio 1 until 1984, often presenting BBC TV's prime chart show, *Top of the Pops*.

1968

OPPOSITE: Senator Bobby Kennedy was gunned down in the early hours of June 6, 1968, by Sirhan Sirhan while leaving a victory celebration at the Ambassador Hotel in Los Angeles after he had defeated Senator Eugene McCarthy in the Californian Primary.

ABOVE: Entertainer Sammy Davis Junior signs the book of condolence following Robert Kennedy's assassination. Kennedy's stance on civil rights was clear when he was Attorney General under his brother Jack and he continued to strongly support racial equality while a senator, touring South Africa in 1966 to support the anti-apartheid movement. His assassin, a Christian Palestinian who bore a grudge against Kennedy for his stance on the Six-Day War, Sirhan was sentenced to death in a Los Angeles court but had his sentence commuted to life in prison.

1968

ABOVE: After 1967's "Summer of Love" came a summer of discontent, with great social unrest across the world. No doubt this was driven by principled opposition to outdated values, but it was also about younger voices making themselves heard. Paris in May 1968 was the epicenter of revolt, begun by student rebellion at the University of Paris and later at the Sorbonne. President de Gaulle's government reacted strongly to the student unrest, closing down the Nanterre campus and introducing a police presence at the Sorbonne. The resulting protest march by students and staff ended in a full-scale confrontation with police, who responded with tear gas and baton charges. It wasn't just the students who were dissatisfied: 11 million workers came out on strike, forcing de Gaulle to call an election in June.

OPPOSITE: A family gathering in 1968 for the Queen's 42nd birthday in the gardens at Frogmore, Windsor. The Queen's children are Charles, aged 19, Anne 17, Andrew, 8, and Edward, 4.

1968

RIGHT: Jim Clark, Formula One driver, sits in his Lotus as mechanics make adjustments to the car setup. Lotus was one of the most innovative racing teams of the time, but their innovations were often tested on the track, with drivers having little practice time. Although the Lotus cars performed well, this was a tragic period for the team, with the death of Jim Clark in April, a crash that nearly killed Graham Hill in 1969, and the death of Jochen Rindt in 1970.

OPPOSITE: Manchester United won the 1968 European Cup final against Portuguese side Benfica. The teams were level at one goal apiece as they entered extra time, but Best, Kidd and Charlton all scored in rapid succession, taking the full-time score to 4–1.

OPPOSITE: Singer Clodagh Rodgers wearing hot pants, which were all the rage in the late 1960s. She achieved some solo success with a couple of chart hits and represented Britain at the Eurovision Song Contest in 1971 before moving to more of a country music style.

RIGHT: Yves Saint Laurent, the French fashion designer, trained at the House of Dior, becoming head designer after Dior's death in 1957 and achieving international fame with his creation of the "trapeze" dress. In 1962 Saint Laurent established his own fashion house where he created many more iconic styles of the 60s including the Piet Mondrian dress, the beatnik look, and "le smoking," a tuxedo for women. He was the first designer to bring out a ready to wear collection.

1968

ABOVE: From January to June 1968 scores of women traveled to London to demonstrate against the Vietnam War. Protesters marched through the streets of the city to publicize their views but most of their actions were centered on Grosvenor Square, site of the United States Embassy, where letters of protest and petitions were frequently delivered. The war finally ended in 1975; the final death toll was impossible to calculate but is estimated at over 2 million, with more than half a million wounded; blanket bombing took a dreadful toll on the civilian population and made it difficult to keep account of the casualty rate.

OPPOSITE: Frightened refugees from the towns and villages around Khe Sanh take shelter from North Vietnamese mortars at the American base.

1968

OPPOSITE: John Noakes (left), Valerie Singleton, and Peter Purves, presenters of the long-running children's TV magazine program *Blue Peter,* host a canine birthday party for the show's pet dog, Petra, who was six.

RIGHT: A United Airlines hostess models their latest uniform. The American company, which had been formed in 1926, had merged with Capital Airlines in 1961, then in 1968 was reorganized to create the UAL organization of which United Airlines was a subsidiary. The new uniforms designed by Jean Louis were much more colorful and more comfortable to wear. Stewardesses were also starting to fight back at contract terms which prevented them from marrying or having children while working for an airline.

1968

ABOVE: A Russian tank invades the city of Prague in Czechoslovakia in August 1968. The countries of the Warsaw Pact had invaded the country to stop Alexander Dubcek's "Prague Spring" reforms. Dubcek's aim had been to reduce the most repressive parts of the communist regime and allow greater freedom of speech and tolerance of organizations not under communist control. The invading forces seized control of the city, taking Dubcek and the other reformers into Soviet custody. They were forced to concede and all except one signed the Moscow Protocol, promising to protect socialism in Czechoslovakia. Dubcek was expelled from the Communist party two years later.

OPPOSITE: Prague residents build a barricade to halt the advance of Soviet tanks using the shells of two burnt-out streetcars.

1968

OPPOSITE: Faye Dunaway and Steve McQueen, two of Hollywood's hottest talents, star together in the clever psychological drama *The Thomas Crown Affair*. Director Norman Jewison used unusual techniques to engage and tease the audience, including split-screen narratives and, as with *The Graduate*, the soundtrack contributed significantly to the success of the movie. "Windmills of Your Mind" won the Academy Award for best song and the movie received two further nominations.

RIGHT: Playwright Harold Pinter began his career as an actor before writing his first play, *The Room,* in 1957. This was followed by classics including *The Birthday Party* and *The Caretaker*. He branched into screenwriting, beginning with the 1963 adaptation of *The Servant* by Robin Maugham, starring Dirk Bogarde and James Fox. In the 1970s he moved into directing, taking on the role of associate director at the National Theatre.

ABOVE AND OPPOSITE: The Biafran War began in July 1967 and lasted until January 1970. The reasons for the war were complex but the human suffering during the blockade of Biafran territory captured the attention of the world. As a dependency of a strong colonial power, Nigeria functioned politically and socially, but after gaining independence from the UK in 1960 difficulties of ethnicity and language surfaced. Biafra's secession from Nigeria was primarily for reasons of ethnicity—but the discovery of substantial oil reserves in the Niger Delta, located in the southeast of Nigeria and included in the territory claimed by Biafra, was an important factor in the conflict. It is estimated that over two million people died as a result of the war, many from starvation and disease.

ABOVE: Lester Piggott riding Sir Ivor races to the line to win the 1968 2,000 Guineas at Newmarket. Piggott also won the Derby with Sir Ivor, who was owned by the US Ambassador to Ireland, Raymond R. Guest; the horse was named for his British grandfather, Sir Ivor Guest. Generally acknowledged to be the greatest flat jockey of his generation, Piggott has recorded 4,493 race wins.

ABOVE: George Harrison with a group of Hare Krishna followers. The Beatles had all become interested in and influenced by eastern, and particularly Indian, mysticism, but George was more drawn to the teachings of the Maharishi Yogi than the others. He also learned to play the sitar, an Indian stringed instrument.

1968

LEFT: Leslie Hornby, using her childhood nickname, Twiggy, became the first celebrated teenage model. Discovered at the age of 16, she rapidly became the face of the 60s after shots of her appeared in the press. After retiring from modeling Twiggy forged a career in acting and singing. A highly acclaimed appearance in Ken Russell's *The Boyfriend* won her two Golden Globe awards.

OPPOSITE: Aretha Franklin won her first two Grammy Awards in 1968, for her 1967 hit "Respect" and Best Female R&B Vocal Performer, and would win the latter the next seven years in a row. Franklin was born the child of a renowned preacher in 1940 and in early childhood displayed extraordinary talent. Recording her first gospel album at 14, it wasn't until 1967, signed to Atlantic Records, that her career took off, and by 1970 she was already regarded as the leading female soul singer.

ABOVE: Mini racing at Silverstone racing circuit, July 1968. Designed by Alec Issigonis at the end of the 1950s, the Mini rapidly became a prestigious symbol of the 60s after the basic Mini was upgraded with a faster engine and a superior braking system. Two models were also designed specifically for circuit racing, and the cars won the Monte Carlo rally three times during the decade.

OPPOSITE: Faye Dunaway and Warren Beatty starred as Bonnie Parker and Clyde Barrow in Arthur Penn's movie *Bonnie and Clyde*, which was nominated for 10 Academy Awards. Beatty was nominated for Best Actor, but he could also take credit for producing the movie, overseeing everything from the script to the final edit.

1969

Recording their final studio album, Let It Be, in 1969 was a double strain for The Beatles, on the brink of splitting up: personal relationships were at a low and the album had been the cause of much wrangling between Paul McCartney and John Lennon; on top of this, to fulfill their three-movie contract with United Artists, the band decided to allow the filming of their studio work as part of the movie Let It Be. To add to the sense of detachment, they were not working in the familiar Abbey Road Studios of EMI but in the new basement studio of their Savile Row, London, HQ. The one major outcome of this tense arrangement was the famous impromptu rooftop performance on January 30, which was halted by police after 42 minutes because of the resulting traffic gridlock. A focal point in the movie, it showed that despite their differences, the Beatle magic had not gone away.

1969

OPPOSITE: Richard Nixon, who had unsuccessfully campaigned for the US presidency in 1960, came to power in January 1969. Here he makes an unscheduled stop to shake hands with Londoners outside Buckingham Palace, where he been to lunch with the Queen.

RIGHT: Richard Nixon seen with British Prime Minister Harold Wilson at 10 Downing Street.

1969

LEFT: *Midnight Cowboy* starring Dustin Hoffman and Jon Voight was directed by John Schlesinger and won three Academy Awards and six BAFTA awards, although it proved controversial with some audiences because of its explicit sex scenes.

OPPOSITE: Robert Redford (left) and Paul Newman in *Butch Cassidy and the Sundance Kid,* which was a critical as well as a box office success; the blend of humor, two of the most dashing young actors in Hollywood, and some great twists, all to a Burt Bacharach soundtrack, won over a generation of movie-goers—and many of those to follow. The picture won four Oscars and three further nominations.

ABOVE: Jeffrey Archer became an MP for the Conservative party in 1969 but stood down in 1974, fearing bankruptcy. A year later Margaret Thatcher appointed him Deputy Chairman of the party but in 2000 Archer was expelled from its ranks after it was revealed he was facing charges for perjury; he was subsequently jailed for four years. A very successful author, his first book, *Not a Penny More, Not a Penny Less*, was published in 1976 and was followed by a string of bestsellers inlcuding *Kane and Abel*.

OPPOSITE: The new Victoria Line was officially opened by the Queen in March 1969. The route stretched from Victoria to Walthamstow and was the first new line to be built for more than 60 years. New features included closed-circuit television and automatic trains and fare collection.

1969

OPPOSITE AND RIGHT: In 1961, inaugurating the Apollo space program, President Kennedy promised that man would set foot on the moon by the end of the decade, and while he would not live long enough to see it, on July 20, 1969, Neil Armstrong descended the ladder of the Lunar Module before a live television audience of about 600 million viewers, and walked on the moon.

1969

OPPOSITE: As children the Gibb family emigrated to Queensland, Australia, where Maurice and his brothers Robin and Barry were soon appearing on television as a singing trio. They returned to England in the mid-60s and were able to secure a contract with Polydor Records. "Massachussets" was their first single to reach number one in the UK. Robin left the group in 1969, although all three reunited in 1970. The brothers co-wrote most of their songs and also wrote for other major artists.

RIGHT: April 23, 1969: pop singer Lulu clutches her Chekov and husband Maurice Gibb of the Bee Gees after their honeymoon in Acapulco, Mexico.

1969

ABOVE: The iconic fashion store Biba was begun by Barbara Hulanicki, initially as a mail order business before a store was opened in Abingdon Road, London, in 1964. On the first day of business the shop had sold every dress by 11 A.M. Five years later all the stock was wheeled down the road to Kensington Church Street; the new premises were nine times larger. Their tumultuous success continued and in 1974 Biba again moved, and was soon attracting a million customers a week. However, the bubble finally burst and the following year the shop was closed.

OPPOSITE: Rock singer Janis Joplin in pensive mood. Joplin was a cult figure by the end of the 1960s, largely because of her powerful vocal performance which enabled her to keep pace with any of her male contemporaries. Her extreme rock and roll lifestyle made her a symbol of liberated woman—but it was her on-off addiction to heroin that would end up killing her: Janis's road manager found her dead in her hotel room in October 1970.

1969

RIGHT: Twenty-five-year-old Tony Jacklin celebrates after winning the 1969 Open Golf Championship, the first Briton to win for 18 years.

OPPOSITE: Quarterback "Broadway" Joe Namath of the New York Jets pictured during a game on September 14, 1969, against the Buffalo Bills at the War Memorial Stadium in Buffalo, New York. In 1969 the Jets surprised the nation by beating NFL champions, Baltimore Colts at Super Bowl III, although Namath himself had been confident of their chances. The Bills had just signed Heisman-Trophy winning running back, O. J. Simpson after his spectacular first two seasons with University of California. Early years with the Buffalo Bills were not impressive and it would not be until the 1970s that Simpson would be able to display the promise of his early years in the game.

1969

ABOVE: Robin Knox-Johnston on his 32ft ketch *Suhaili* sailing toward Falmouth at the end of the first *Sunday Times* Golden Globe round-the-world race in 1969. Of the nine sailors that started, Knox-Johnston was the only one to complete the course and become the first man to sail single-handed around the world non stop, completing the distance in just over 10 months. He achieved this feat three more times during his sailing career and was awarded the CBE in 1969.

OPPOSITE: The end of the 60s and the end of the Locarno dance hall, its neon sign flashing for the last dance.

1969

ABOVE: American GIs cautiously approach a South Vietnamese girl and woman during a search for Vietcong weapons in Thuam Long, December 1969.

OPPOSITE: Soldiers of the First Cavalry Division descend from a Chinook helicopter into thick bush near the Cambodian border.

1969

OPPOSITE: Cass Elliot, better known as Momma Cass of The Mamas and the Papas, runs through a soul medley with Tom Jones on his TV show in March 1969. *This Is Tom Jones* was a British ATV production but it was networked in the USA by ABC. Tom Jones was one of Britain's most successful musical exports to the USA in the late 1960s.

RIGHT: Folk duo Simon and Garfunkel in concert in 1969. Their contribution to the 1968 movie *The Graduate* and its release as an album was quickly followed by the hugely successful album *Bookends* the same year. At the 1969 Grammy Awards the pair were awarded Record of the Year for "Mrs Robinson" while Simon received a personal Grammy for Best Original Score. Sadly the duo were moving apart, even while recording their bestselling album *Bridge Over Troubled Water,* which was released the following year to huge acclaim and more Grammys. Simon and Garfunkel broke up in 1970.

1969

ABOVE: Hunger strikers sit at "Free Derry Corner" underneath a mural, painted in 1969, announcing the entrance to the Bogside area of the city.

OPPOSITE: Israeli premier Golda Meir, who came to power in March 1969, meets with British Prime Minister Harold Wilson. Meir would lead Israel through a number of crises while in office, including the massacre of the Israeli Olympians at the Munich Games in 1972 and the Yom Kippur War in 1973. She died in 1978, aged 80, from cancer.

1969

ABOVE: Charlie Watts, Mick Jagger, Keith Richards, Bill Wyman and Brian Jones formed the Rolling Stones in 1962 with Jagger and Richards making up the main songwriting partnership. In 1969 Mick Taylor (left) replaced Jones, who drowned in his swimming pool. shortly after leaving the band.

OPPOSITE: In the late 1960s, British television steadily moved over to color broadcast. When programs were not being aired, a test card was broadcast instead: BBC engineer George Hersee's daughter, Carole, provided what would turn out to be an iconic image for the color test card for BBC TV for nearly four decades. Here London region commercial channel Thames TV recreates the test card scene.

1969

ABOVE: Actor David Hemmings during rehearsals for role as a racing driver. Hemmings rapidly established himself as a sixties pin up appearing in films including *Blowup*, *Charge of the Light Brigade*, *Camelot*, and the cult film *Barbarella*, directed by Roger Vadim.

OPPOSITE: Jackie Stewart raced in Formula One from 1965 to 1973, winning the Drivers' Championship three times—1969, 1971, and 1973— and earning himself the nickname "The Flying Scot." After a crash in 1966 he fought tirelessly for improvements in the safety at racetracks, both for spectators and drivers, and many compulsory measures in place today are a result of Stewart's campaigning.

1969

RIGHT: Diana Rigg, playing the character of Tracy, and George Lazenby as James Bond, rehearse a scene from *On Her Majesty's Secret Service*, released in 1969. Lazenby followed on from Sean Connery playing the main character but only appeared in one film. Connery appeared in the next production before Roger Moore took over the prestigious role.

OPPOSITE: Actor Roger Moore pictured with his new wife Luisa Mattioli in April 1969. Moore first made his name in television, most notably in his portrayal of Simon Templar in *The Saint*. He then starred alongside Tony Curtis in *The Persuaders!*, earning £1 million for one series, giving him the status of the highest paid television actor in the world at the time. *The Persuaders!* was followed in 1973 by the Bond movie *Live and Let Die*, the first in a 12-year career as the renowned secret agent.

ABOVE: On the night of July 18, Senator Edward Kennedy drove his car off a bridge at Chappaquiddick Island into the water below. Kennedy fled from the scene, but his passenger Mary Jo Kopechne died in the crash. He failed to report the accident, only contacting the authorities after her body was discovered the following morning. After pleading guilty to leaving the scene of an accident Senator Kennedy was given a two-month suspended sentence.

OPPPOSITE: John Wayne's appearance in the 1939 Western *Stagecoach* had established him as a star, but he won his only Oscar for his portrayal of the ageing, one-eyed marshal Rooster Cogburn in the classic Western *True Grit*.

ACKNOWLEDGMENTS

Written and edited by:
Tim Hill; Gareth Thomas; Murray Mahon; Marie Clayton; Duncan Hill; Jane Benn; Alison Gauntlett; Alice Hill

****

The photographs in this book are from the archives of the Daily Mail. Thanks to all the photographers who have contributed and the film and television companies who have provided Associated Newspapers with promotional stills.
Every effort has been made to correctly credit photographs provided. In case of inaccuracies or errors we will be happy to correct them in future printings of this book.

Thanks to all the staff at Associated Newspapers who have made this book possible. Particular thanks to Alan Pinnock.
Thanks also to Steve Torrington, Dave Sheppard and Brian Jackson.

Thanks to the many Associated Newspapers photographers who have contributed including:
John Knoote, Steen, G Talbot, Phillip Jackson, J Twine, Stilling, George Elam, J. Silverside, Crispian Woodgate, Raymonds, L. Joseph, Beverley Goodway, Smart, R Fortune, Mike Burnett, Monty Fresco, Roger Bamber, Bryan Jobson, Ronald Spencer, James, Claude Parnall, Rossetti, Bill Johnson, Ling, Hart, Shaw, Jimmy James.
With contributions from associated photographers: Peter Arnett, Henri Huet, David Farrell, Rick Merron.

Additonal photographs courtesy Getty Images
Art Rickerby, Time & Life Pictures pg 147; Lee Lockwood, Time & Life Pictures pg 248; Cecil Stoughton, Time & Life Pictures pg 82-83; AFP/Getty Images, pg 28 pg; Bob Thomas/Getty Images pg 29; Keystone, Getty Images, Hulton Archive pg 42 pg 146; Diamond Images/Getty Images pg 48-49; Ernest Sisto, Getty Images, Hulton Archive pg 98; Sydney O'Meara, Getty Images, Hulton Archive pg 116; Victor Drees, Stringer, Getty Images, Hulton Archive pg 117 pg 136; CBS Photo Archive, Getty Images, Hulton Archive pg 138; Michael Ochs Archives, Getty pg 140-141; RacingOne/Getty Images pg 176-177 pg 270; Slava Katamidze Collection, Getty Images, Hulton Archive pg 204; STF, AFP/Getty Images pg 232; Herb Scharfman/Sports

Imagery, Getty Images North America pg 226-227 pg 242; Fred Mott, Fred Mott, Getty Images, Hulton Archive pg 249; Kidwiler Collection, Diamond Images/Getty Images pg 278-279; Roy Jones, Hulton Archive, Getty Images pg 310-311; Lambert, Getty Images, Hulton Archive pg 312; Tony Duffy, Getty Images North America pg 317 pg 319; Popperfoto/Getty Images pg 318;Reg Lancaster, Hulton Archive, Getty Images pg 328; Tony Tomsic, Getty Images North America 364

Courtesy NASA: 78-79 and 358 (also used on the cover montage)

Film and Television:
Psycho, Shamley Productions Paramount/Universal   13; The Apartment, United Artists/Mirisch 30; Cleopatra, Twentieth Century-Fox 31; West Side Story, United Artists/Mirisch 44; La Dolce Vita, Riama/Pathe 45; The War Lover, Columbia 93; The Great Escape, United Artists/Mirisch 112; It Happened at the World's Fair, Metro-Goldwyn-Mayer 122; Doctor in Distress, The Rank Organisation, 123; The Pink Panther, United Artists/Mirisch 132-133; Goldfinger, United Artists/ Eon Productions 156, 157; Dr. Who and the Daleks, British Lion/Regal/AARU Productions 211; Lilith, Columbia Pictures 277; The Good the Bad and the Ugly, PEA   266; In the Heat of the Night, United Artists/Mirisch 282; You Only Live Twice, United Artists/Eon Productions 296; Half a Sixpence, Paramount/Ameran Films 297;Bonnie and Clyde, Warner/Seven Arts/Tatira/ Hiller Productions 349; Midnight Cowboy, United Artists 354; Butch Cassidy and the Sundance Kid, Twentieth Century-Fox Campanile 355; On Her Majesty's Secret Service, United Artists/Eon Productions/Danjaq 379; True Grit, Paramount Pictures 381; Hancock's Half Hour, BBC 21; Dr Kildare, BBC, Arena Productions 53; Take Your Pick, Associated-Rediffusion Television 52; The Dick Van Dyke Show, BBC, Calvada Productions 64-65; Coronation Street, Granada Television 69; 145; Bonanza, BBC, NBC 118; The Week That Was, BBC, Leland Hayward Productions 127; Basil Brush, BBC 139; Bewitched, ABC, Ashmont Productions, BBC 144; The Black and White Minstrel Show, BBC 190; Thunderbirds, ATV, AP Films 191; Till Death do Us Part, BBC 238; The Man from U.N.C.L.E, BBC, Arena Productions, NBC 269; Gilligan's Island, BBC, CBS 300

Published by Transatlantic Press
First published in 2010

Transatlantic Press
38 Copthorne Road
Croxley Green, Hertfordshire
WD3 4AQ

© Atlantic Publishing
For photograph copyrights see pages 382–3

A catalogue record for this book is available from the British Library.

ISBN 978-1-907176-00-5

Printed in China